CARVING LARGE BIRDS

Bill Dehos & Patrick Spielman

Sterling Publishing Co., Inc.   New York

ACKNOWLEDGMENTS

The authors express their sincerest gratitude to Mary and Peter Charles, Peter Bauer, and Lee Edmunds for allowing us to photograph and include their various big birds. Others who contributed and helped include Bob Spielman, Hot Tools, Inc., and our excellent typist, Julie Kiehnau.

Edited by Barbara Busch

Library of Congress Cataloging-in-Publication Data

Dehos, Bill.
  Carving large birds.

  Includes index.
    1. Wood-carving—Technique.   2. Birds in art.
I. Spielman, Patrick E.   II. Title.
NK9704.D37   1986   731.4′62   86-14436
ISBN 0-8069-4742-X (pbk.)

CONTENTS

INTRODUCTION

This book presents a practical, middle-of-the-road approach to the essential how-to's involved in carving a variety of large birds. The ideas and content presented here are not intended to be a more advanced or demanding art form than decoy carving. The problems are just different. The carving of big birds requires different information, different types and sizes of tools, and wood. The realistic decoy carver is a perfectionist. He strives to copy every detail; every feather line is perfect. Often these carvers work from stuffed models, attempting to create a realistic, live-looking copy. This sort of wood carving is very regimented. The majority of these carvers might look at a carving with a crack in the wood as being completely hopeless.

On the other end of the carving spectrum are those carvers who work in crude lines with virtually no detailing at all. Chain-saw carvers and similar wood carvers might fit into this category. They do their carving fast. They are not concerned about cracks because they prefer a rustic carving.

The approach in *Carving Big Birds* is somewhere between the extremes. The carvings represent more boldness and more freedom than those of the realistic decoy bird carver. The examples in this book show more of the nature of the wood being expressed in the carving, but they also exhibit a very definite feeling that thought and effort is put into the work.

Carving is a process of skill and enjoyment. The objective should be to enjoy the entire process. The more thought, time and energy you put into it, the better the finished product will be and the greater the satisfaction and sense of achievement you will have at the completion of each carving.

One of the most enjoyable aspects of carving is involved in finding and cutting your own wood. You will receive a sense of excitement when you find an unusual or special piece of wood. It then becomes fun to find or think up an idea for a special carving to utilize the features of that special piece. It's especially satisfying to find something that nature seems almost to have especially provided for you. It's a serendipitous feeling!

Creativity involves seeing something through from start to finish. Today, with all of the plastics, metals, assembly lines, factories and big complex organizations, it's nice to create something of value and beauty—from your own personality and love—something that never would exist if it weren't for you, and which you and others will enjoy for many years to come. Enjoy nature, exercise your mind, and create something of aesthetic value with your own hands. The excitement will come when ideas, material, and skill all merge in a spirit of freedom with boundless variations and possibilities; that's what carving is all about!

It is hoped that this book may be an inspiration to would-be carvers of large birds. All you need are a few tools, green or dry chunks of logs, a little patience, and a lot of determination. Don't be afraid of mistakes or be concerned about cracks. You will be surprised at how much you and others will appreciate your work even if it isn't perfect. You might have fun and surprise yourself.

This book is intended to broaden the wood carver's scope and provide an interesting departure from the monotonous routine of a highly technical, mechanized society. We've included many step-by-step examples to assist you in making some beautiful and dramatic sculptures of life-sized big birds. Majestic eagles, graceful swans, herons, a flamingo, various owls, and the rugged features of hawks are included in photos and multi-view drawings. It is our hope that this book will start you on your way to countless hours of pure enjoyment and deepen your love and affection for wood, the ultimate sculpturing material.

1
TOOLS
AND BASIC
TECHNIQUES

The birds illustrated in this book were carved with just a few basic tools. Although not all of the tools illustrated are absolutely necessary, you will find their use advantageous as a convenient time saving because large quantities of wood need to be removed when carving many of the "big birds."

A *chain saw* (Illus. 1) is practically a necessity if you intend to cut up trees for your material. A lot of stock can be removed quickly with the chain saw during the early, roughing out stages of producing a carving. The use of a chain saw is illustrated frequently throughout the book. However, handsaws and chisels or other power tools can be used for roughing out the carvings if so desired. The primary advantage of using a chain saw to rough out carvings is simply speed and convenience.

Illus. 1.   An inexpensive electric chain saw is available with different length cutting bars, which can be as short as 8 inches long.

A small, inexpensive electric chain saw, as shown in Illus. 1, is available at most hardware dealers. This offers the advantage of convenience in maneuverability and handling because of its light weight when compared to the heavier gas-powered chain saws. Other advantages of electric chain saws are: 1) You can start and stop easily by using the trigger switch. 2) They are good for indoor use because of their lack of exhaust smoke. 3) They are easier on the ears—they run more quietly than gas-engine saws. Manufacturers are also changing the design of saws and the cutting chains to improve their overall safety. However, if you're a novice, it would be prudent to get some personal, hands-on safety instruction from some knowledgeable individual, such as from a chain-saw dealer or experienced logger. Always study and observe the manufacturer's safety recommendations for not only chain saws, but all other hand and power tools as well.

One safety feature of chain saws well worth investigating is a newer style of chain that is designed to minimize kickback or bucking tendencies which can be very dangerous with a chain saw. Notice the guard link design, in Illus. 2, which tips out as the chain travels around the end of

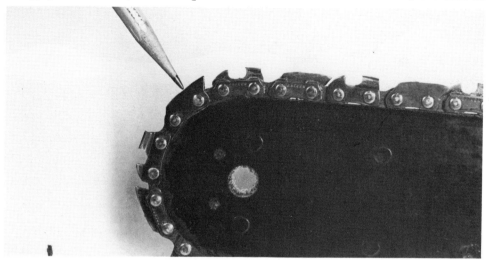

Illus. 2. A chain designed to minimize the kickback or bucking. This chain with the "guard link" appears to be safer than the standard cutting chain shown in Illus. 3.

the bar. This reduces or controls the amount of bite when cutting with this area of the bar. A standard chain is shown in Illus. 3 for a visual comparison. Turn to pages 28, 117, and 158 for just a few of the illustrations included in this book that show roughing-out work with the chain saw.

Illus. 3. A look at the standard style cutting chain.

A *bandsaw* (Illus. 4) is certainly a timesaving piece of equipment, although it is expensive. Bandsaws are especially good for cutting laminated stock because it is usually dry wood and it has at least one flat surface. In preparing stock for laminating, jointers, planers, other saws, clamps, and so on are sometimes required or at least helpful. However, the bandsaw is probably one of the most important machines for anyone carving the big birds of this book.

Illus. 4. A bandsaw is a good tool to have when making large birds. The machine shown can cut stock 12" thick and easily cuts the top and side profile shapes quickly.

A *die grinder* (Illus. 5) or some other powerful rotary tool is extremely useful and a practical consideration for the serious carver. The one shown in the photo rotates at 25,000 rpm and it will accept various cutters and burrs that have ¼″ diameter round shanks.

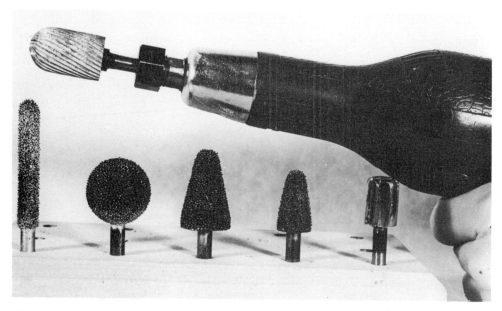

Illus. 5.   This ¼″ high-speed die grinder is a powerful, fast cutting tool. Structured carbide bits below, with steel burrs, at far right, and in the tool above, were the cutters used most often on the carvings in this book.

Illus. 5 also shows the basic set of cutters used. The structured carbide cutters are ideal for working in tight areas, on burls, and the like. You do not have to always be concerned about cutting "with-the-grain" when using such cutters, as you do when using knives, chisels and gouges.

Illus. 6.   Using the die grinder to form sculptured feathers.

The die grinder is another tool that is essentially a roughing tool, but it can be used to make various surface textures such as the carved feathers shown in Illus. 6. In fact, most surfaces can be shaped with this tool, but smooth flowing surfaces of beautiful woods require extra sanding to achieve a finish worthy of the carving.

Power sanders (Illus. 7) are other convenience tools. You can always sand by hand! Carving big birds always requires some hand-sanding in "tight areas" anyway. So, when convex or other surfaces are conducive to power-sanding, time and energy will be saved. It should be noted, too, that sanders are used to do much more than just smooth. It would be reasonable to say that sanders are used about equally for final shaping as

Illus. 7. Power sanders.

well as for initial smoothing. The disk sanders are used to smooth out the rough surfaces made from chain-sawing (Illus. 7) and some of the surfaces worked with the die grinder. The larger disk sander in Illus. 8 carries a very coarse abrasive 36 to 50 grit and the drill attachment (shown in the same photo) carries an 80 or 100 grit abrasive. The circular sanding marks left from the disk sanders are taken out with the small pad sander and by hand.

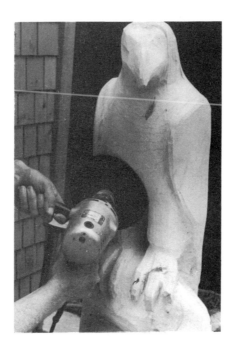

Illus. 8. Disk sander is used for rough-shaping and sanding where applicable.

Hand edge tools (Illus. 9 and 10) show carving chisels, gouges, carving knives and whatever other type of edge tools you feel comfortable with. The tool sets shown in Illus. 9 are just suggestions, but fairly essential ones in our opinion. Many of the birds shown in this book can be carved without owning all of these tools. If you so desire, the incisions that simulate feather texture (Illus. 10) can be made in two angular passes with a blade knife or in one pass with the v-tool as shown.

Illus. 9.   Essential carving tools. Small sizes at left, standard-size tools at right with mallet above, and homemade carving knife below.

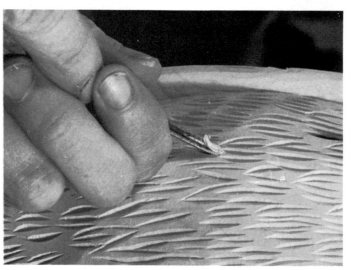

Illus. 10.   Small parting tool is very practical for feather texturing and similar work.

Carving knives are an area of possible controversy that we don't want to get too deeply into. Today, there are literally hundreds of different blade and handle configurations available for carvers to choose from. Use what suits your taste and experience best. Bill likes his own homemade knife with the longer blade, and Pat prefers his small, commercially made knife. Both are shown in Illus. 11.

Illus. 11.   Special self-made knife, top, is ground from an old straight razor and epoxy glued into an oak wood handle. Compare to commercially available carving knife bottom.

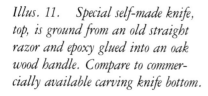
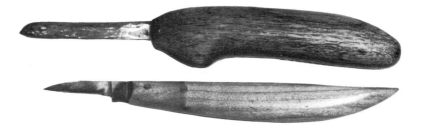

A *woodburning tool* (Illus. 12) is very useful. Use it to deepen and darken lines in outlining feathers, to shade the pupils of eyes (Illus. 13) or for shading areas such as the surfaces of a bird's claws or talons (Illus. 14). Turn to page 31 which shows the burning tool used to sign the carving and to page 29 which shows the burning tool for making simulated annular rings in the end of a carved log base.

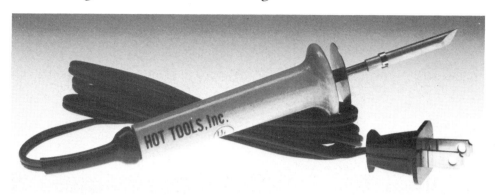

Illus. 12.   *Typical woodburning tool.*

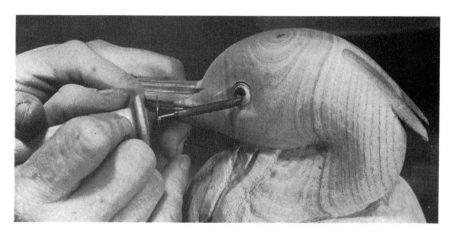

Illus. 13.   *Eye shading with a burning tool.*

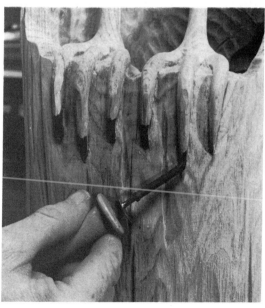

Illus. 14.   *Coloring and shading the hard-looking surfaces of the bird's claws with a woodburning tool.*

Other tools used to make the birds in this book include hand or electric drills, clamps, and vises, and some very special tools designed and made by author Dehos for forming carved eyes and texturing bird claws. Turn to page 25 and 30, respectively, for more information concerning these easy-to-make devices.

WOODS

Assuming you have some tools, you have to be motivated to take the first step. That is to go out and obtain some wood.

At first thought, the idea of securing pieces of wood in large sizes suitable for carving big birds would seem to present some very serious problems. Not so. There is a very common-sense approach to this problematic subject. Just getting suitable wood is a stumbling block that often discourages and prevents wood carvers from creating anything with some size to it. The answer is to use a common, locally available species of wood directly from the tree. You can even consider those woods that are not normally used for carving or wood crafting.

Usually, the beginner worries more about cracks than does the experienced carver because he is more used to accepting them. When it comes right down to it, in order to have a good supply of carving wood, it is best to have a lot of it cut. Allow nature to dry it over whatever period of time it takes, which may be a year or more for some woods. It's a good idea to cut dead or partially dry trees when possible to speed the drying process. With a plentiful supply of cut wood you can pick and choose those pieces that are most suitable for the carving you have in mind. Thus, size needs and the location of defects on the respective pieces can be considered for a specific carving. This is a far better approach than cutting only one piece and putting all of your hopes and work into it.

Roughing-out a carving removes a large amount of the wood which will reduce bulk, reduce stresses and reduce the depths of existing cracks. If you take a green log and rough out a carving, it will dry faster and with shallower cracks than the whole log. Sometimes wood will not start cracking until the wood is almost dry. When you bring a piece indoors into the dry winter's artificial heat for its final drying stages, it may tend to crack. The best thing to do is just go ahead and carve. If cracks appear at this point or later in the curing or drying stages you will just have to accept them. Be positive, luck will be on your side or if cracks appear they probably will not be all that disappointing. The impact of a carving and its overall shape is not destroyed by a crack. In fact, a crack often enhances a carving.

Sometimes you can even find better and far more interesting wood than you can buy. It depends on how hard you look and search for it. In fact, sometimes it's free just for the sawing or hauling. The wood available locally may be quite a bit different than clear chunks of wood you might buy or laminate together to make flawless pieces.

If you're willing to accept some conditions that might otherwise be classified as defects, you will find an abundance of carving wood in any forest, wood lot, firewood pile, or even in your own backyard. True, you

Illus. 15.   This quail carving is a vivid example of wormy butternut. It sits on an ironwood "knob."

may have to contend with conditions such as wormy wood, knots, dead limbs, decay-hollowed sections, cracks and splits. But don't panic! Look at the many examples in this book to see how some of Mother Nature's effects can be used to create special points of interest or unique qualities to the carving. Illus. 15 shows a bird carved from wormy butternut. The wormy woods have become more popular in recent years. As a rule wormy woods do not crack or split as readily as do other pieces of woods in the same species.

As can be seen in Illus. 16, knots do not seriously detract from a carving, unless they are located in undesirable areas, such as near an eye or on the beak in which case it would make the carving more difficult or structurally weak. Knots, even a decayed one, on the back side or in the base of a carving often do more to make the piece interesting than anything else. Cracks and checks (Illus. 17 and 18) are hard to predict where they might develop. As a general rule harder and denser woods tend to be more brittle and have greater tendencies to crack. Most often, slicing a big log into halves or quarters with a chain saw greatly reduces cracking possibilities. Some woods are hard and heavy but they seem to be tough. A huge elm, for example, may not crack very much because its cell or grain structure appears to be somewhat interwoven. Another general feeling is that knotty woods seem to crack less overall than do clear pieces of the same species. It's best to observe your wood as you allow it to dry (3 months to a year) after cutting. If cracks develop, it's usually possible to work around them. Store your wood supply in the shade, in a protected area off the ground. Dead or fallen trees often have existing cracks that are either fully open or the log will indicate with some checking where major cracks may develop later. It becomes a skill

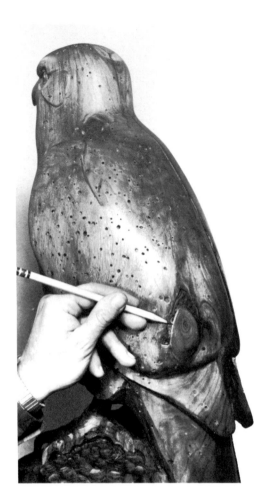

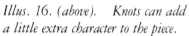

Illus. 16. (above).   Knots can add a little extra character to the piece.

Illus. 17. (above right).   Do not be overly concerned about cracks in the wood. Even a large crack, as shown here, is a part of the nature of wood.

Illus. 18. (right).   Here is another crack that does not weaken the structural qualities of the carving. On a base, cracks are often more acceptable.

Illus. 19.   Should this crack be objectionable, if it's reasonably straight, wedges can be fit and glued in. See Illus. 20.

Illus. 20.   Tapered wedges of the same species of wood are cut with the table saw to the appropriate sizes. They are glued in and carved to conform to the existing contours.

when selecting which part of a particular chunk of wood should be made into the front, side, and so on of the bird. In case a crack should open up, it can be left as nature intended it to be or you can fill it (Illus. 19 and 20).

Some of the kinds of woods used for the birds in this book include just a few of the many different kinds of wood available in northeast Wisconsin. White cedar is a good wood for outdoor carvings and some of the birds were laminated from cedar planks to make up larger chunks for carving. Butternut is one of this area's favorite woods. It is a dependable carving wood with a very pretty figure and color. It has good stability and also gets wormy. See the color section.

Walnut is nice if you can find it, although it tends to crack easier in chunk form than many other woods. It is a beautiful dark brown color and it finishes nicely. We think it is best for accents and inserts. White ash has a darker heartwood and black ash is of a rich, brown coloring.

Black cherry is recommended for smaller carvings. It is reddish brown in color. A number of the larger birds were carved from box elder. This is a wood usually held in low regard by most carvers and woodworkers. However, we think the results were very satisfactory and almost spectacular. Box elder is a creamy color with reddish streaks, a very striking combination. Other woods used in lesser degrees include ironwood, which produces some beautiful burly bases. Staghorn sumac, a rich golden yellow wood, is sometimes available in sizable chunks.

The list of suitable woods could go on and on. The important thing is to look to the wood that is near you. Be on the watch for trees and stumps left when clearing wooded areas for housing developments, road construction, and trimming done in parks or the clean-up of fallen trees from storms, and so on. Illus. 22 shows how to cut up a tree. Notice how crotches, dead or broken limbs, and so on can be worked effectively into the various kinds of big bird carvings. Be sure to analyze and study the possibilities before you start sawing.

The alternative to working directly from the tree is to laminate by gluing layers of boards or planks together. This produces stock that is more predictable with less cracking and more over all stability than chunks cut directly from a log or tree (Illus. 21).

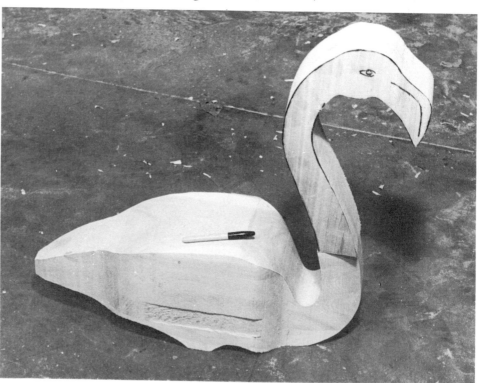

Illus. 21.   A laminated body that has been compound-sawn to create this rough shape. Note the size of this bird in comparison to the pen in this photo. Also note the vertical grain on the long neck and head member.

In addition to gluing together pieces to increase the size of the wood, it is common practice to join and glue parts together so that the grain of the individual parts or pieces will provide the greatest amount of strength possible (Illus. 23 and 24). Usually joint strengtheners such as dowels are required to effect enduring joints where changes of grain directions are necessary. Typical examples of birds with areas where dowel joints were used are illustrated in Illus. 21, 23, 24, and 25.

Illus. 22. Drawing, showing how to cut up a tree to get reusable pieces of wood for bird carving.

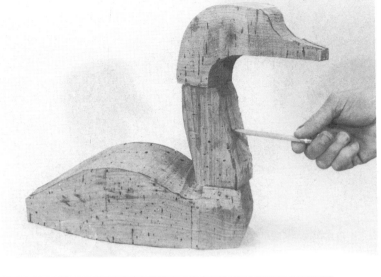

Illus. 23.   On birds with long vertical necks, prepare the stock blanks so that the grain runs with the longest dimension or the length as shown here. Refer to page 48 for a gluing and clamping illustration for making this western grebe.

Illus. 24.   Gluing, as in this neck-to-body assembly, often requires some clamping ingenuity.

Illus. 25.   To maintain durability of the carving throughout the curvature of the head and neck, the joint shown here was necessary. The joint was dowelled.

Inserts involve anything where a piece is set into a prepared opening to eliminate the problem of "short grain." Inserting a beak is one method of changing the grain direction to an abrupt right angle. See the example in Illus. 26. Crests and other feathers are often carved from inserts in decoys. The same idea can apply to large birds as shown in Illus. 27.

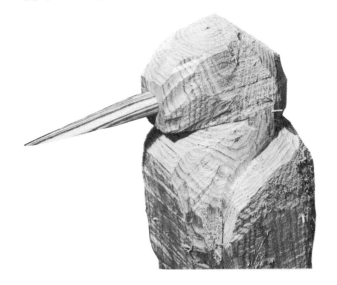

Illus. 26.   The beak is glued into a bored hole during the rough carving stages and then it is carved to final shape and size.

Illus. 27.   The tips of the crests would be extremely delicate unless made as the inserts with the grain direction shown here.

Beaks require several different techniques in carving. In addition to the inserted beak, shown in Illus. 28 and 29, on some birds the head and beak can be carved from the same piece of wood. The eagle head shown in Illus. 30 is a good example. The beaks on most of the birds in this

Illus. 28.   For obvious strength requirements, the beak is best set into the head as shown.

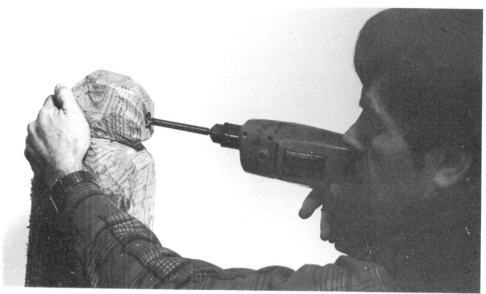

Illus. 29.   Boring a hole for an inserted beak should be "eyeballed" carefully so that the beak will be straight.

Illus. 30.   One-piece head and beak. Although the grain runs vertically the design of the beak presents sufficient bulk; consequently, the strength is adequate.

book are carved from the same piece as the head. The design and grain of the wood is such that there aren't serious "short grain" problems as there would be on the heron if the beak and head were carved from the same piece. Various details can be highlighted, shadowed, or colored effectively with the woodburning tool after all carving and sanding is completed. See Illus. 31.

Illus. 31.   Using the burning tool to define the line separating upper and lower mandible.

Carving the *eyes* into the head is a whole lot easier than it looks. We've included some easy-to-make tools that almost make eye carving a "snap." Carved eyes are preferred over the use of the glass inserted eyes that are commonly used in decoy carving. Carved eyes appear much more artistic, and are in keeping with the integrity of a sculpted wood carving. In short, they are not so artificial looking, but appear more natural.

First carve the eye area so it conforms to the general contour of the head, as shown in Illus. 32. Emphasize the bony ridge over the eyes of eagles, hawks, and most birds of prey, though not owls (Illus. 33 and 34). Eyes can also be inserted as shown in Illus. 34 and 35. The large eyes of owls (Illus. 36) are easy to carve with a knife and gouge. If carving is of wormy wood, simplify the details, and avoid the eyelids and so on.

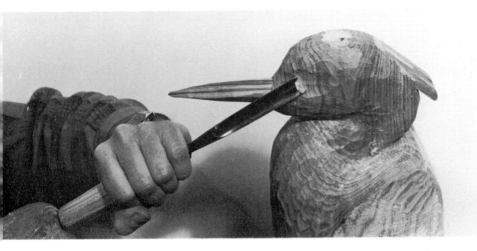

Illus. 32.   Use a gouge or the die grinder with a burr to sculpt the eye area.

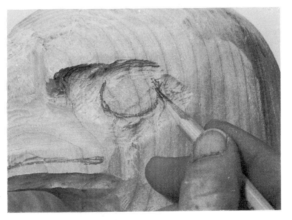

Illus. 33.   Pencil in the eye before carving to preview its appearance and location.

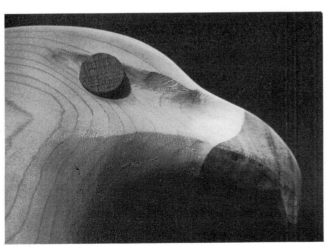

Illus. 34 and 35.   Round dowel (or plugs) of a contrasting wood makes an impressive eye.

Illus. 37 and 38 illustrate some effective techniques applied to hand-carved eyes with some added details such as eyelids, and shaped pupils. Notice that the eyeballs are not perfectly round. Do not try for perfection. It's the effect that's important, not the accuracy or precise proportion.

Illus. 36.   This hand-carved round eye is about as simple as can be.

Illus. 37 and 38.   Closeup examples of two hand-carved eyes. Note one is more rounded (actually for an eagle) and the other is slanted for a different effect on an owl.

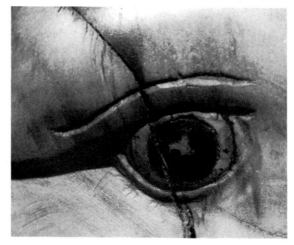

Eye-forming tools (Illus. 39 and 40) are easy to make and they are ideal for the beginning carver. Simply cut a 2 to 4 inch length of mild steel rod.

Illus. 39.   Self-made eye-forming tools, in various sizes, cut convex surfaces representing the eye. This type maintains the integrity of a wood carving—making it more sculptural than using the usual inserted glass eyes.

Illus. 40.   Eye tool in use is powered with a portable electric drill, preferably rotating at a slow speed.

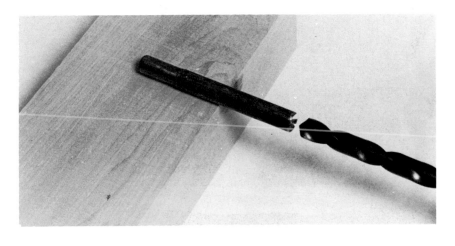

Illus. 41.   Making eye-forming tools is easy. Simply drill into the end of mild steel rod as shown here.

The diameters of the rod should equal the desired eye size. With a regular high-speed steel drill of the same diameter, drill into the end of the rod on its center as accurately as possible (Illus. 41). Drill only to a depth that produces a sharp rim around the end of the steel rod (Illus. 42). Use a triangular file and make a cutting lip for chip removal. Eye-

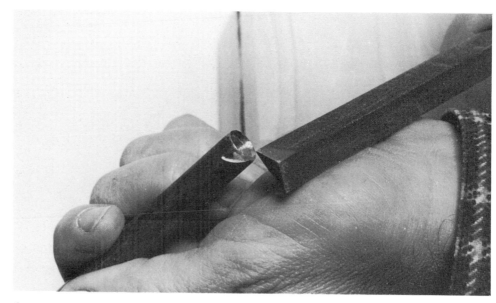

Illus. 42. To complete the eye-forming tool, file a "lip" as shown with a triangular file.

forming tools of any size can be made in this manner. A set including: ¼, ⁵⁄₁₆, ⅜ (or ⁷⁄₁₆), and ½ inch will form most of the eyes in this book with the exception of the larger owl eyes which are mostly hand-carved. However, the forming tools can be used to define the pupils of these eyes as well. Illus. 43 is a good example.

Illus. 43. Another eye technique where the eye-forming tools were used to define the pupils.

Illus. 44 illustrates the use of several different sizes of eye tools used to make one eye on a heron. Illus. 45 shows how effective a couple of basic slicing cuts can be applied to make the "corners" of an eye on a loon. The surfaces of the pupil can also be shaded. Carefully, work the woodburning tool over the appropriate areas of the pupil to achieve a very alive, realistic look. Illus. 46 shows that the entire surface *is not* shaded.

Illus. 44.   Eye-forming tools of several different diameters were used to give this eye its specific effect of lid, iris and pupil.

Illus. 45.   Another eye technique. The eye is carved with the eye tool and the corners of the eye are cut with a sharp knife or gouge.

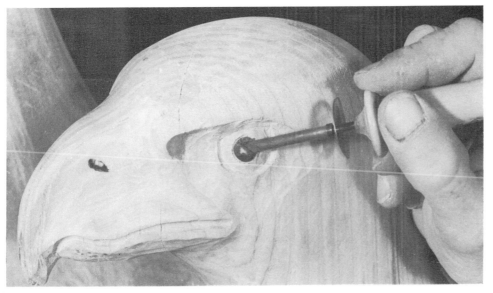

Illus. 46.   Using the burning tool to shade the pupil of an integrally carved eye.

For *feet and bases*, it is essential for most carvings that the bird be standing or effectively supported. Consequently, the feet need to be carved as if standing or clutching some other creature. Almost every carving with such bases are made with the bird and base carved from one piece. The roughing-out operation is very important and it's almost

Illus. 47.   This shows a roughed-out bird, the roughed-out legs and feet on an integral base which will also have a carved fish in the clutches of the bird.

Illus. 48.   This base will eventually be carved to look like a log. The spots are oil splatters from the chain saw.

Illus. 49.   Carving chisels are used for preliminary shaping.

Illus. 50.   Carved bases can be given a very natural look with a properly located carved knot, as shown here.

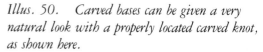

like planning and making two carvings in one. Illus. 47 and 48 graphically illustrate roughed-out birds with their feet and the integral bases. Preliminary roughing of the feet or claws begins with a gouge or chisel. Illus. 49 shows the shape starting to develop. Feet and claws are carved simultaneously with the base so that all the details come together effectively. See Illus. 50, which shows the claws ready for the final smoothing-out operation. Illus. 51 will give you an idea for creating a dead branch or cleaning up a real one. The woodburning tool can be, again, an effective tool. Illus. 52 shows its use in shading the surfaces of the claws, and Illus. 53 shows how the end of a carved log was textured with woodburned annual rings and simulated checks.

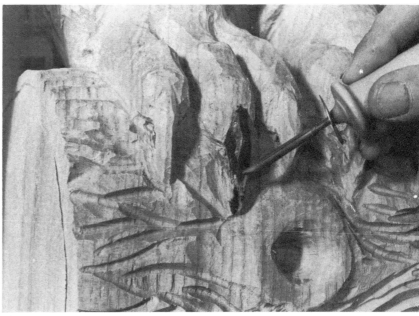

Illus. 51. (above left).   Effective techniques in making bases include carving knots, bark textures, and hollow, dead branches as shown here.

Illus. 52. (above right).   Using the woodburning tool to shade claws.

Illus. 53. (left).   This unusual base is not a natural log. It is carved to look like a log with bark, knots, branch, end grain, and checks—all special effects.

Carvings having big, thick, or massive bases should be hollowed out to reduce bulk and reduce weight (Illus. 54). However, more importantly, hollowing relieves stresses, speeds drying, and minimizes checking and cracking. Illus. 55 looks into a base deeply hollowed with the chain saw.

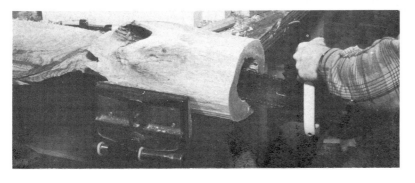

Illus. 54.   Hollowing a base with the chain saw.

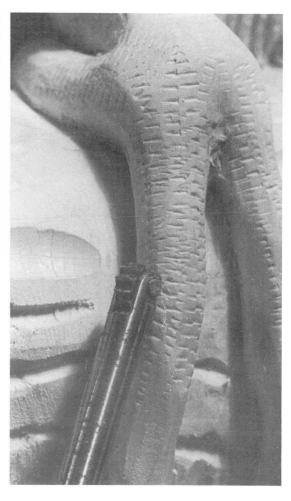

Illus. 55.   A hollowed-out base, as shown, reduces weight and relieves many of the stresses that might cause cracking and checking to the carving.

Illus. 56.   Self-made tool for texturing bird feet and legs. It is made from ⅛" mild steel, wheel-shaped, about ¼" in diameter with about 11 or 12 edges filed sharp. This was set into a slot cut into the end of an old screwdriver shank. It was pinned with a nail axle and peened.

The surfaces of the feet on some birds are textured or patterned with surprising regularity. A homemade tool for embellishing or embossing leg and feet surface textures is shown in Illus. 56. When pressure is applied, the tool rolls along embossing the surface producing a very desirable effect. The wheel is made from ⅛" mild steel and shaped to about ¼" diameter. The wheel is worked with a file to make 11 or 12 sharp edges. This small star-like wheel is set into a slot cut into the end of an old screwdriver shank. It is pinned with a nail axle and peened.

Steel legs and feet can also be fashioned from metal. In some cases, the steel has great strength advantage over wood. This is especially true on birds, such as herons, that have spindly legs. Claws can be ground and filed to tenacious points, toes can be cold bent and welded together as shown in Illus. 57. In this illustration the metal used was concrete reinforcement rod (or "re-bar"). This is available from most building-supply dealers in various sizes.

Illus. 57.   Close-up of steel bird foot, arc-welded.

Illus. 58.   A light wood, such as cedar, shown here, can be colored any one of several different shades with pigmented danish oil. This finish is a deep penetrating stain and finish all in one. It is not overly pigmented to obscure the feather outlines and other details wood-burned into the surface.

Illus. 59.   All carvings should be signed and dated—another use of the wood-burning tool. Notice the hollowed base.

Finishing involves all of those operations that follow final sanding. This includes woodburning details, feather outlines, as shown in Illus. 58 (if desired), and signing your name to the bottom (Illus. 59).

Most of the birds in this book were finished naturally, as opposed to being painted with heavily pigmented coating materials such as paint, enamels, or acrylics. The danish penetrating oils are available in a variety of semi-transparent pigmented color tones. They are very easy to use. Soft woods, such as cedar (Illus. 58) absorb more finish than do denser woods like ash (Illus. 60).

Illus. 60.   Finishing the denser hardwoods such as ash, shown here, may produce lighter shades than the same finish applied to softwoods.

Illus. 61.   Thinned-out paints allow the grain of the wood to show through. It's important that just enough be applied so a subtle rather than harsh color results.

Sometimes a yellowish or white-like effect is desired, such as when finishing sea gulls or the heads and tails of eagles. This is not very specific, depending upon the hardness of the wood and if it is side grain or end grain, but to some extent oil-base pigmented artists' oils or house paint can be mixed with danish oil. It's a good idea to experiment and test on similar scrap surfaces. Wipe the surfaces after allowing the finish to soak for a length of time, depending upon the intensity of the color desired.

EDITOR'S NOTE:
Patterns for some of the birds were too large to reproduce in this book. They have been reduced, therefore, and printed on top of a grid, showing the correct scale ($\frac{1}{2}'' = 1''$, $\frac{3}{8}'' = 1''$, $\frac{1}{4}'' = 1''$ and $\frac{3}{16}'' = 1''$). Patterns can be enlarged or reduced simply by using squares of the appropriate size. Draw the same number of squares as are given on the original. Make the pattern by reproducing the lines and drawing in each corresponding square, one at a time, until the pattern is reproduced to the desired size.

Bald eagle, one-piece carving (including carved log base), finished with dark danish oil finish.

A

B

Opposite page: Bald eagle with brown trout. Stained box elder with lacquer finish.

Golden eagle, carved in white cedar with inset walnut eyes, walnut bill and with a dark danish oil finish.

Close-up of the golden eagle head. Note walnut eyes and bill.

C

Common loon in wormy butternut.

Cinnamon teal in natural butternut.

Bobwhite quail of wild cherry on a box elder base.

D

Ring-necked pheasant of wormy butternut on black ash base.

Pileated woodpecker, rough-textured white cedar with wood-burned details.

Top left: Broad-winged hawk, in natural butternut, standing on one leg.

Top right: Broad-winged hawk in walnut with a rat in its talons.

Left: Peregrine falcon or duck hawk in butternut.

F

Broad-winged hawk, black ash crotch, natural oil finish.

Goshawk carved from one piece of wormy butternut.

Brown pelican of laminated white cedar with dark danish oil finish.

Dwarf penguin in solid butternut.

Opposite page: Herring gull in stained laminated white cedar.

Above: Barred owl, in one-piece wormy butternut, grasping a dead screech owl.

Right: Barn owl, carved in wormy butternut, with field mouse.

J

Right: Horned owl clutching a cottontail rabbit. All carved from one piece of box elder and with a natural oil finish.

Below: Great horned owl, holding a red squirrel, in natural butternut.

K

Scarlet macaw, one-piece carving in box elder, with lacquer finish.

Flamingo of laminated white cedar.

Parrot in one-piece box elder with clear lacquer finish.

Two blue herons: one to the right has steel legs.

Whistling and mute swans of white cedar with wood-burned details.

2
BIRDS AND PLANS

The Bobwhite Quail

Bobwhite quail are ground-dwelling game birds with cheery calls. They build their nests on the ground. Quail eat insects, seeds, berries, and such. The chicks can fly a few days after hatching, and they are fully grown in just eight weeks. At night, a bevy of quail lie in a circle, heads pointing outward so they can spot an enemy's approach and fly away.

Illus. 62.   Bobwhite quail of
cherry on box elder base.

Illus. 63.   Front view of quail.

Illus. 65.   Tail detail on quail.

Illus. 64.   Top view of quail.

Illus. 66.   Quail head. Note
wood-burned beak and eye.

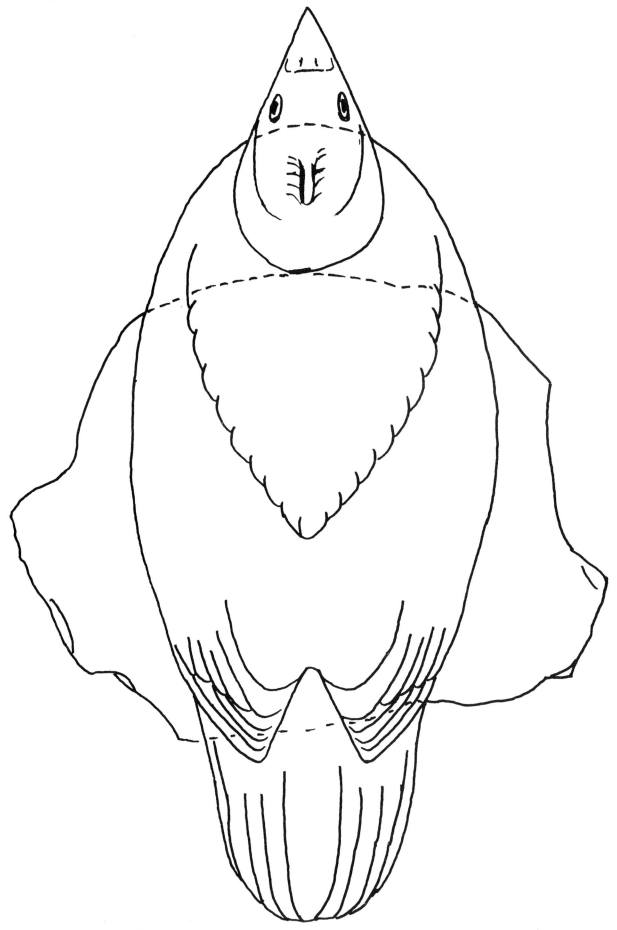

Illus. 67.   Pattern of bobwhite
quail, top view. 1" = 1"

Side view.

The Ring-Necked Pheasant

Ring-necked pheasants were originally imported from China. The males are colorful game birds, the tails are long, narrow, and pointed at the end with eighteen feathers. One species has become the domestic chicken. Pheasants frequent the margins of woods and feed in the open on grains, berries, seeds and insects.

Illus. 68.   Ring-necked pheasant.

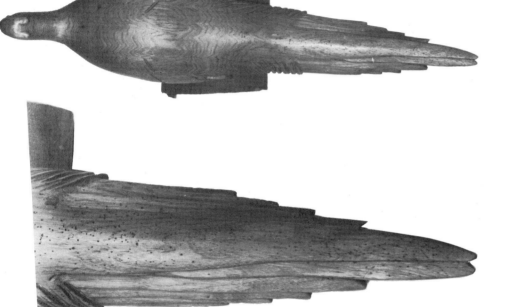

Illus. 69.   Pheasant—top view.

Illus. 70.   Tail, top view.

Illus. 71.   Underside of tail. Note the hollowing effect.

Illus. 72.   Side view of long tail feathers.

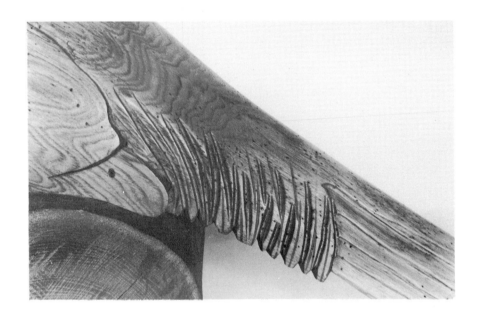

Illus. 73.   Another close-up.

Illus. 74.   Pheasant head close-up. Eye is glass, 10 or 11 mm special.

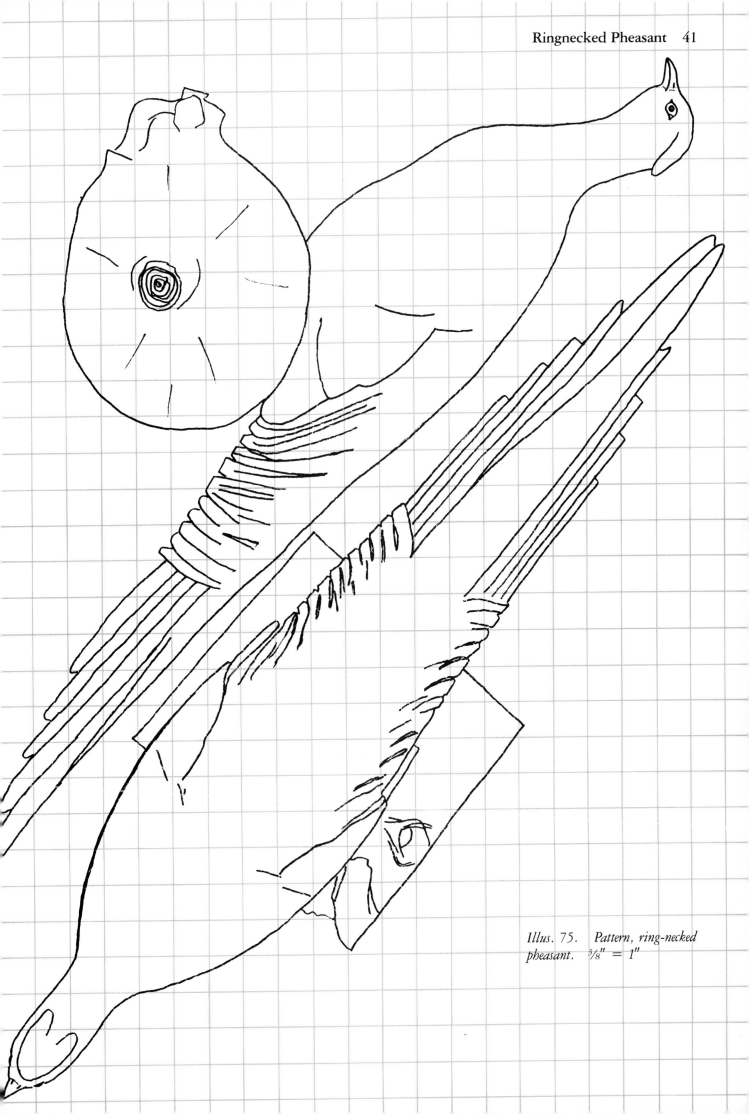

Illus. 75.   Pattern, ring-necked pheasant. $3/8'' = 1''$

The Common Loon
(or Great Northern Diver)

Common loons are large birds with unearthly cries. Loons have their webbed feet positioned far back on their body, and have a clumsy walk on land. They have eighteen or twenty short, stiff, tail feathers. Their nests are hollows or made of grass, moss, reeds and mud. They are very good divers and feed mostly on fish. They probably have the same ancestors as do gulls.

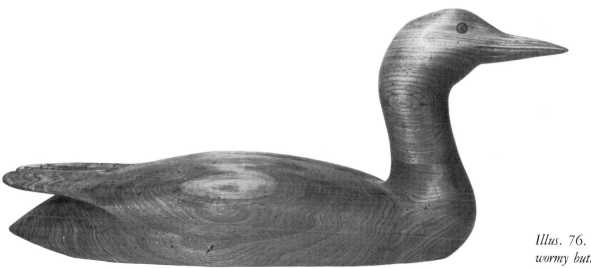

Illus. 76.   Common loon, in wormy butternut.

Illus. 77.   Loon, side view.

Illus. 78.   Loon, wing tips.

Illus. 79.   Close-up of loon head.

Illus. 80.   Another view of the head.

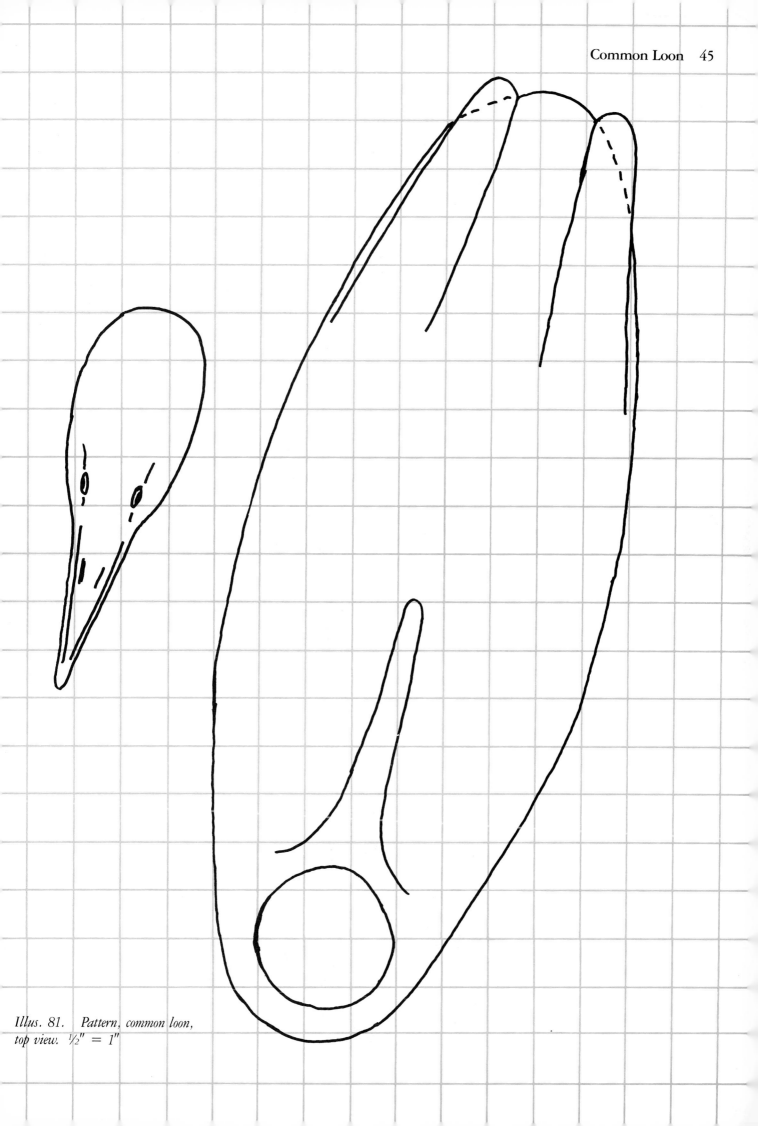

Illus. 81.   Pattern, common loon, top view. $\frac{1}{2}'' = 1''$

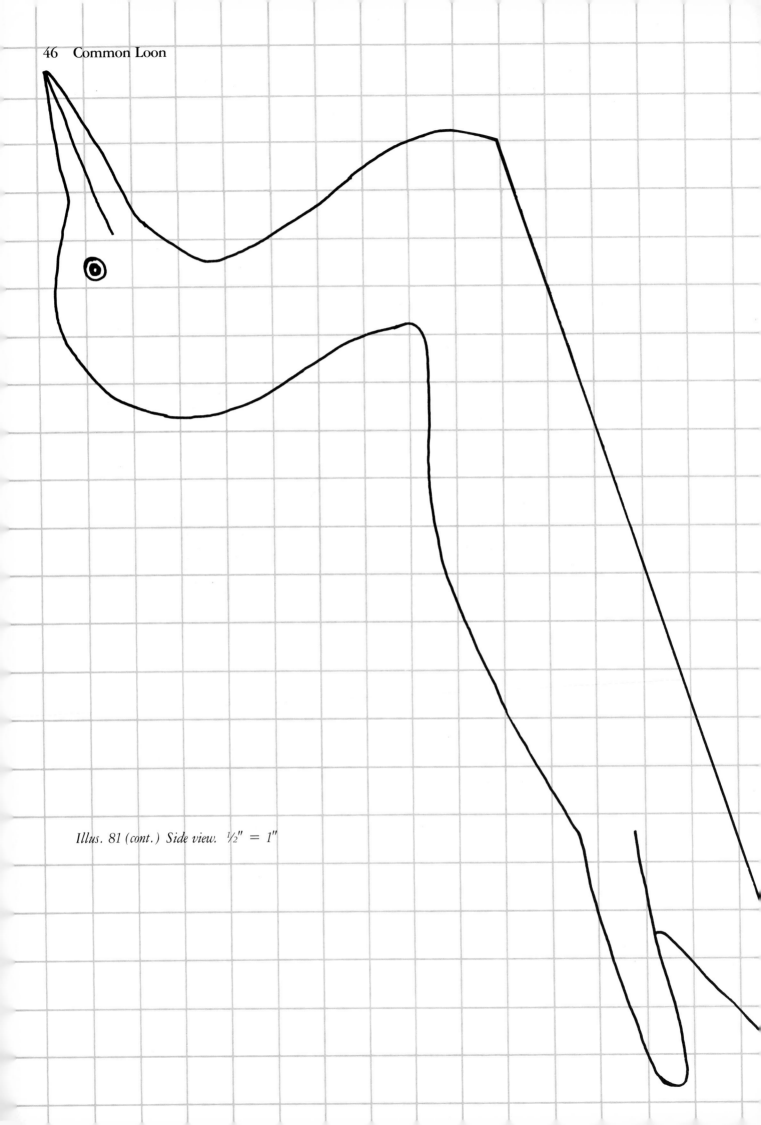

Illus. 81 (cont.) Side view. ½" = 1"

Western Grebe (Running Grebe)

The western grebe's neck is nearly as long as its body, and they are sometimes called swan grebes. They are good swimmers and divers and carry young chicks on their backs. They breed in colonies. Their nests are raft-like structures of plants and reeds. Grebes feed on aquatic bugs, insects, fish, and other animals and vegetable matter. They also swallow feathers for some reason. Grebes have lobed feet, located far back on the body.

Illus. 82.   Western grebe in wormy butternut.

Illus. 83.   Gluing neck and head to body.

Illus. 84.   Rough blank of grebe. Note grain direction runs with neck and is dowelled and glued to head and body pieces.

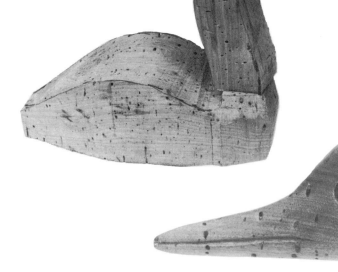

Illus. 85.   Grebe, head close-up.

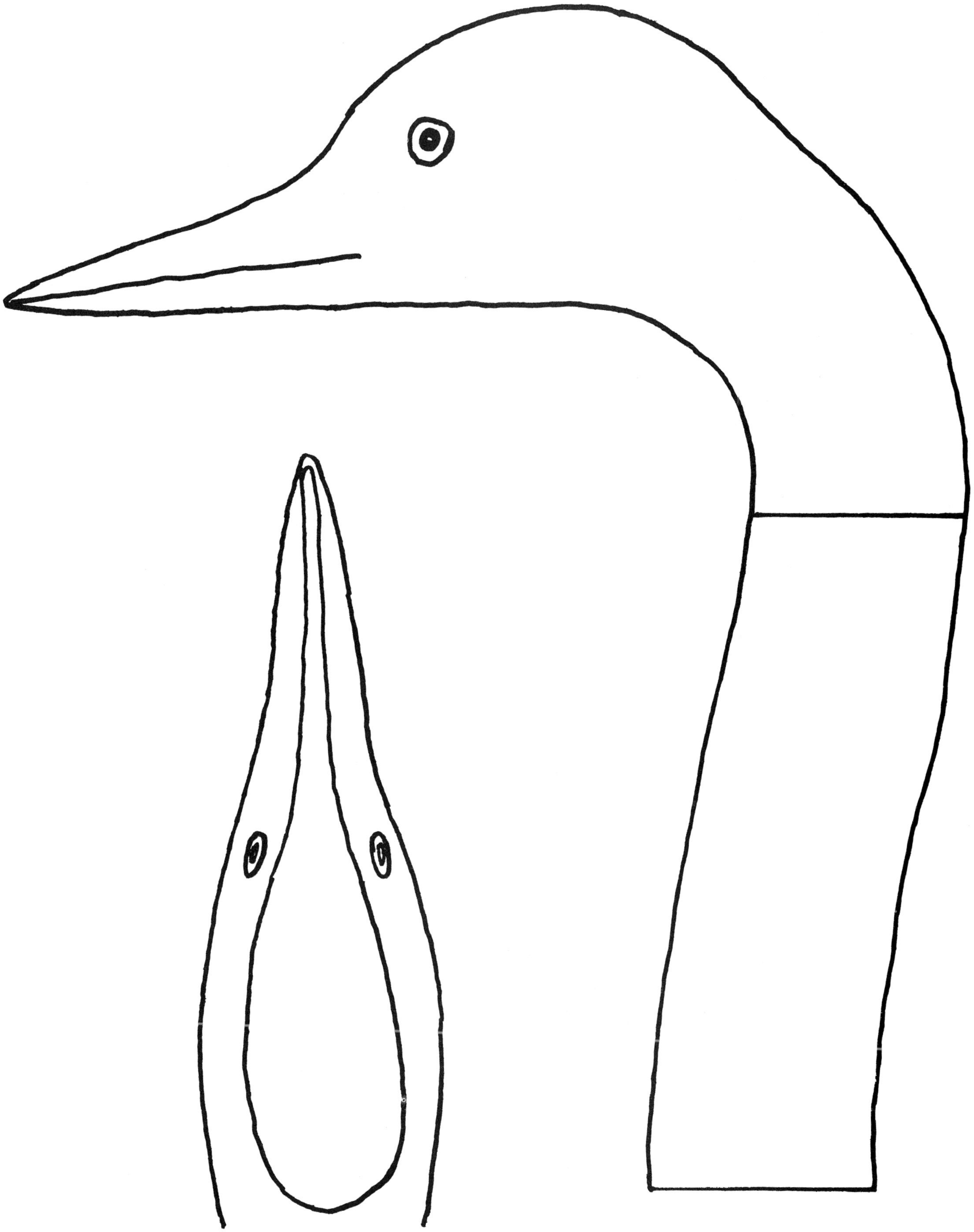

Illus. 86.   Pattern, views of head, western grebe. 1″ = 1″

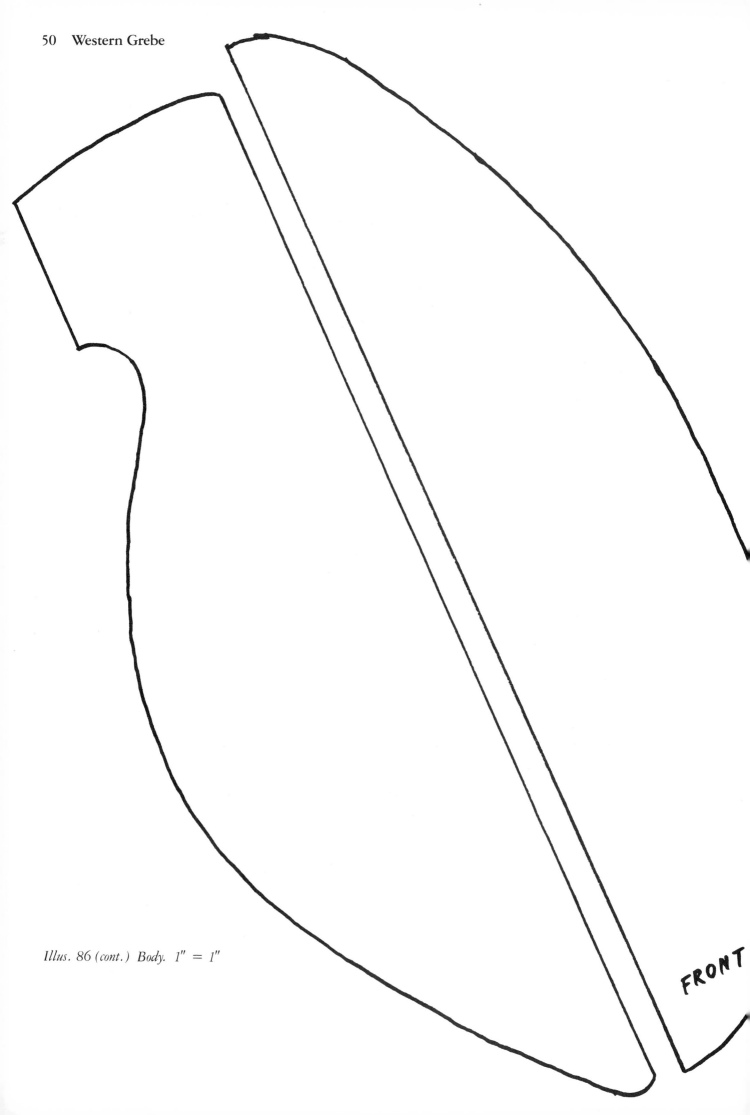

Illus. 86 (cont.) Body. 1″ = 1″

FRONT

Herring Gull

Herring gulls' front toes are webbed and they swim
readily. Like all gulls, herring gulls are voracious, are
mostly beachcombers, fond of carrion and eat garbage.
They almost always breed near the water. Gulls are
gregarious birds and their nests are grass or among
boulders and rocks. Gulls have great flying skills with
their long pointed wings. All gulls certainly add an
aesthetic quality to landscapes.

Illus. 87.   Herring gull of laminated cedar, carved dowel legs, oil stain finish. Glass eyes 12 mm yellow, woodburned feather, and beak outlines.

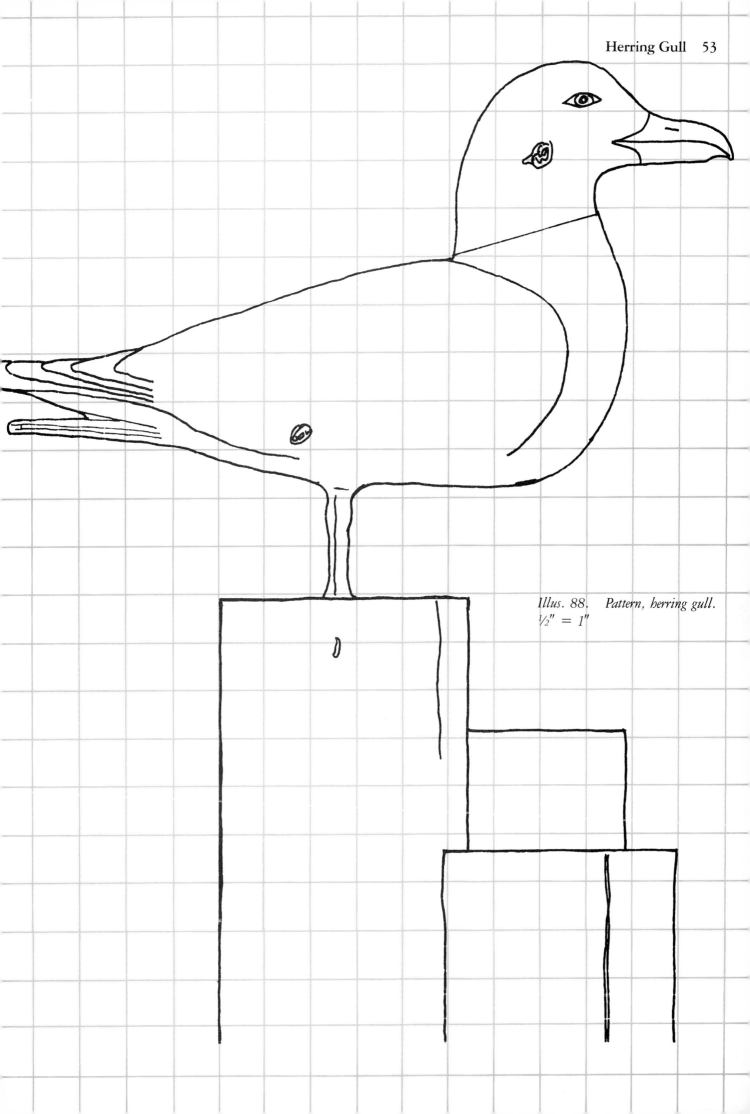

Illus. 88.   Pattern, herring gull.
½" = 1"

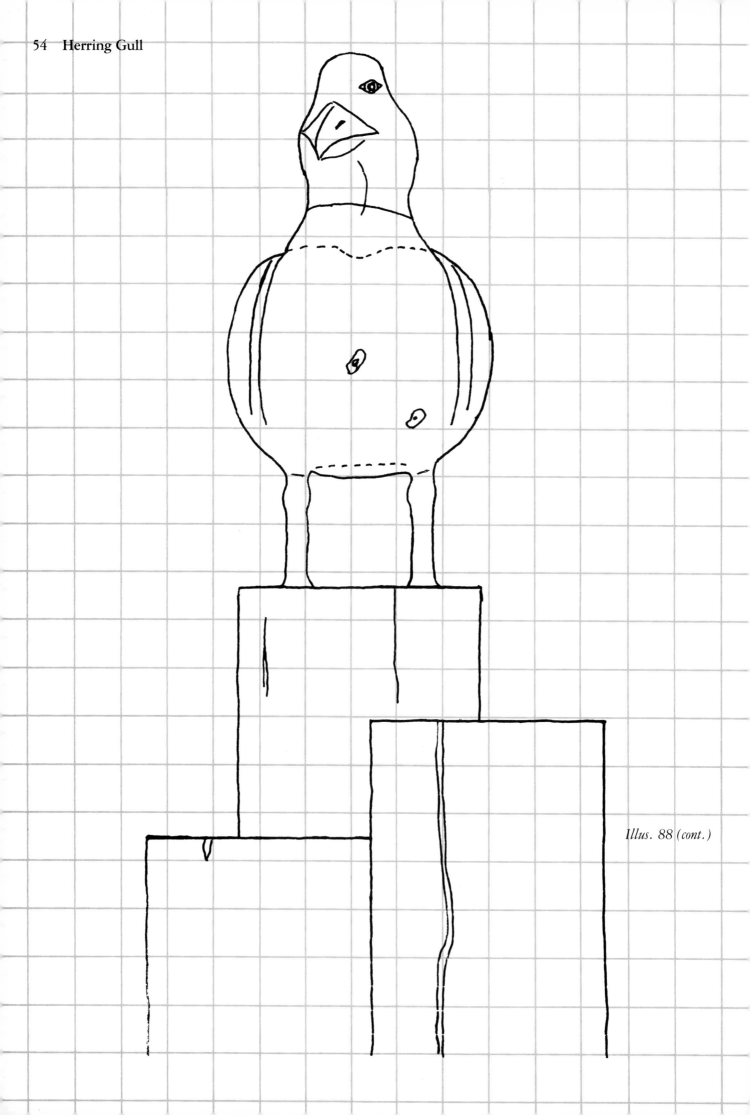

Illus. 88 (cont.)

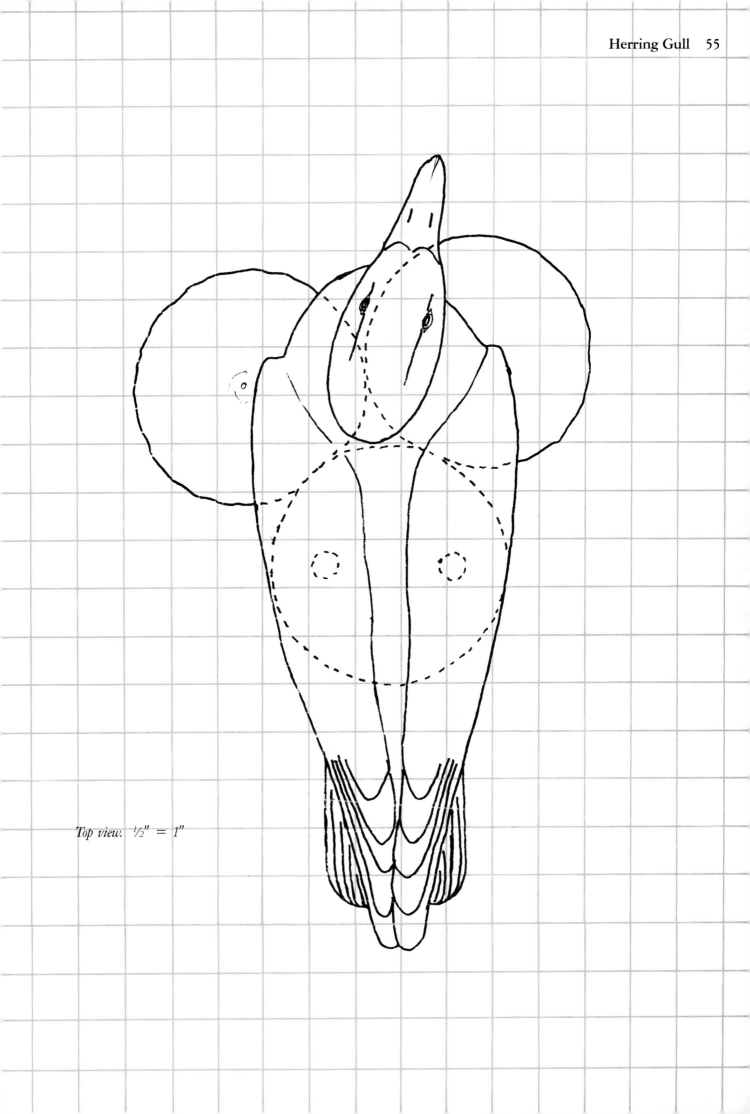

Top view. ½" = 1"

Pileated Woodpecker

P ileated woodpeckers usually nest in cavities in trees which they hollow out with their large, powerful beaks. They have four toes, two pointing forward and two pointing back. Most of their food, consisting of grubs and insects, is found in the bark and the deadwood of trees. It is a large, impressive bird. The ivory-billed woodpecker is the only one larger than the pileated.

Illus. 89.   Pileated woodpecker carved in cedar on hollow cedar post.

Illus. 90.   Side view, woodpecker.

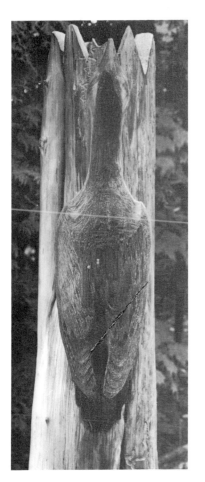

Illus. 91.   Back view of wood-pecker.

Illus. 92.   Head close-up of wood-pecker. Beak is carved from an inserted birch dowel. Eye detail accentuated by woodburning.

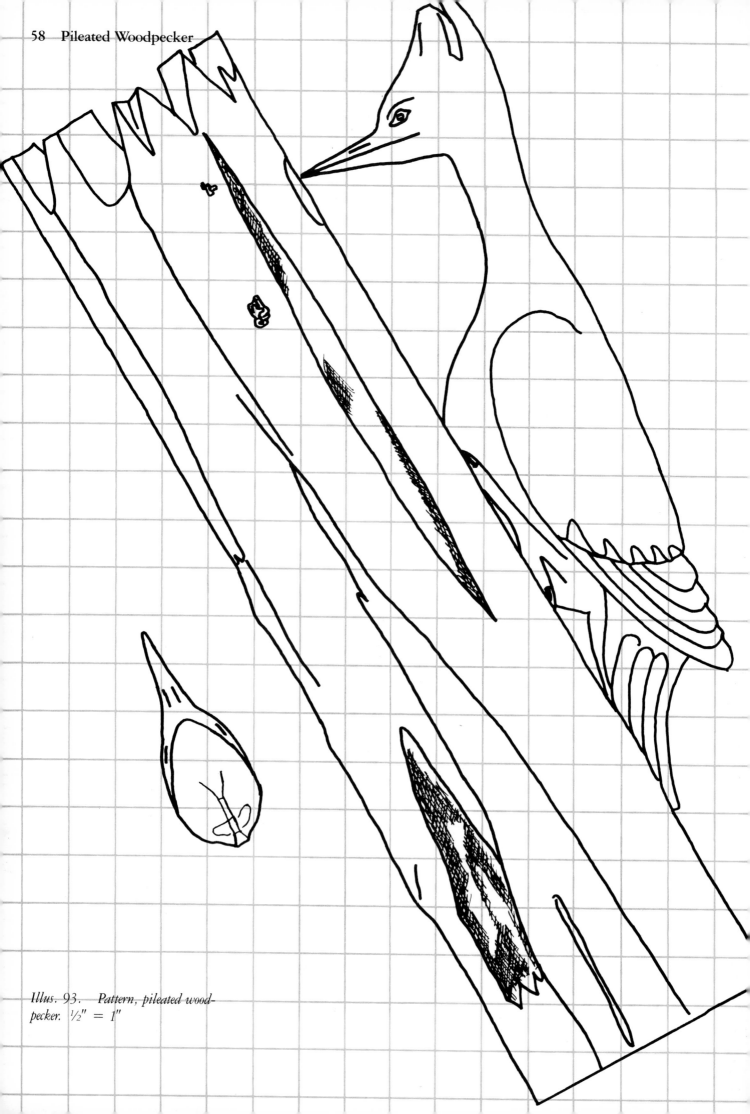

Illus. 93.   Pattern, pileated wood-
pecker. 1/2" = 1"

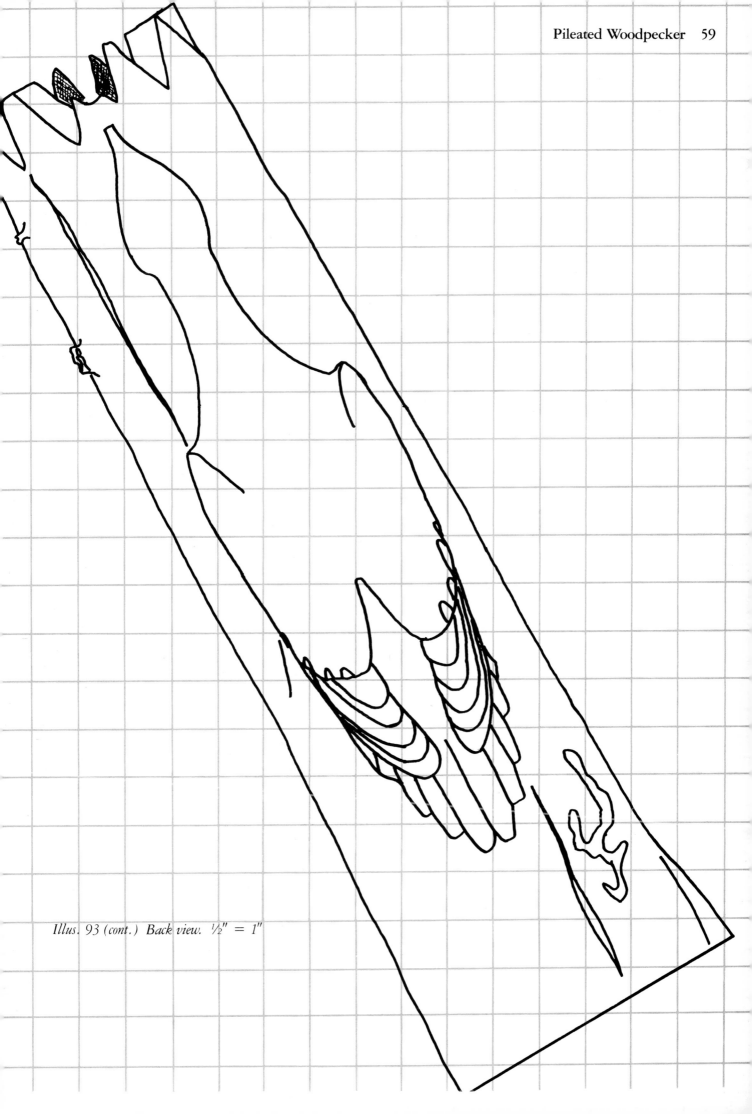

Illus. 93 (cont.) Back view. ½" = 1"

Mute and Whistling Swans

Swans are large water birds with long necks, which may be longer than the body. Swans are graceful and very elegant birds. Both sexes have similar, white plumage. The nests are made of grass, reeds, moss, and other vegetable matter. Their food is mainly seeds and vegetable matter. The young are called cygnets.

Illus. 94.   Mute swan carved from solid cedar log. Note crack which adds to charm of this carving.

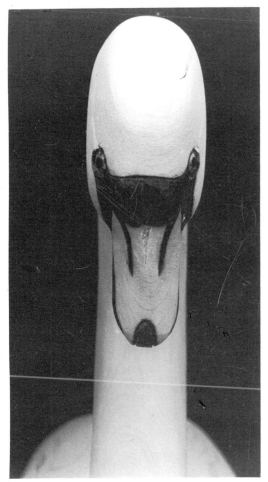

Illus. 95–97.   Various head views of mute swan.

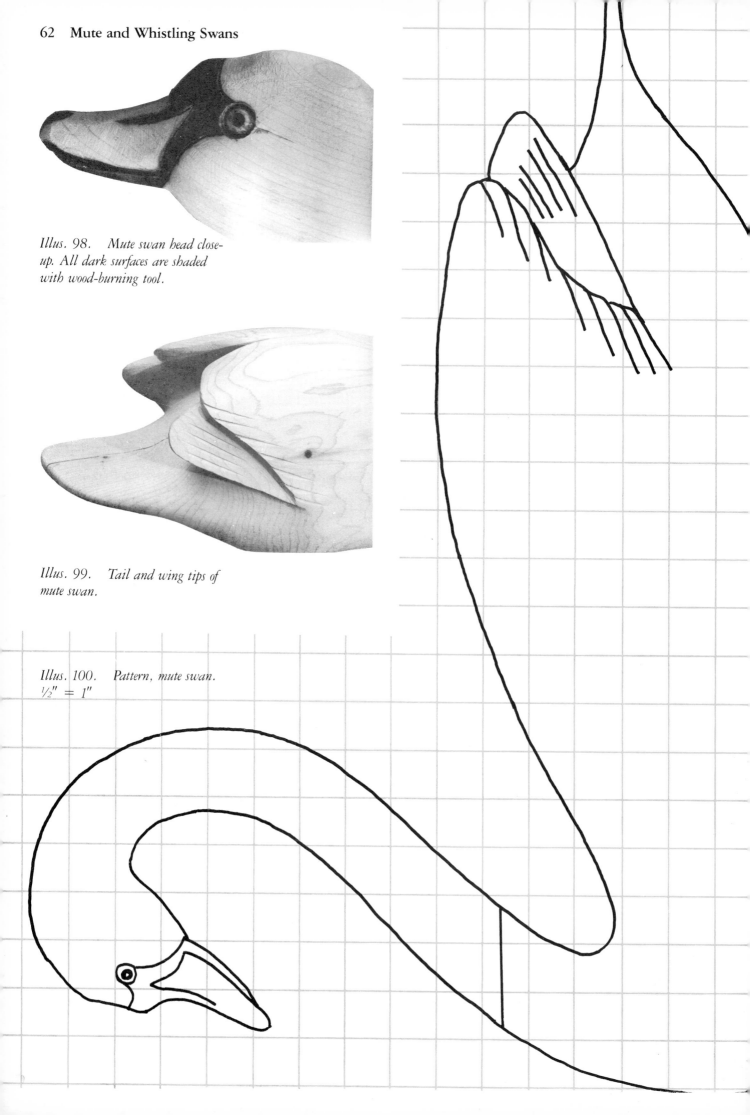

Illus. 98.   Mute swan head close-up. All dark surfaces are shaded with wood-burning tool.

Illus. 99.   Tail and wing tips of mute swan.

Illus. 100.   Pattern, mute swan.
½″ = 1″

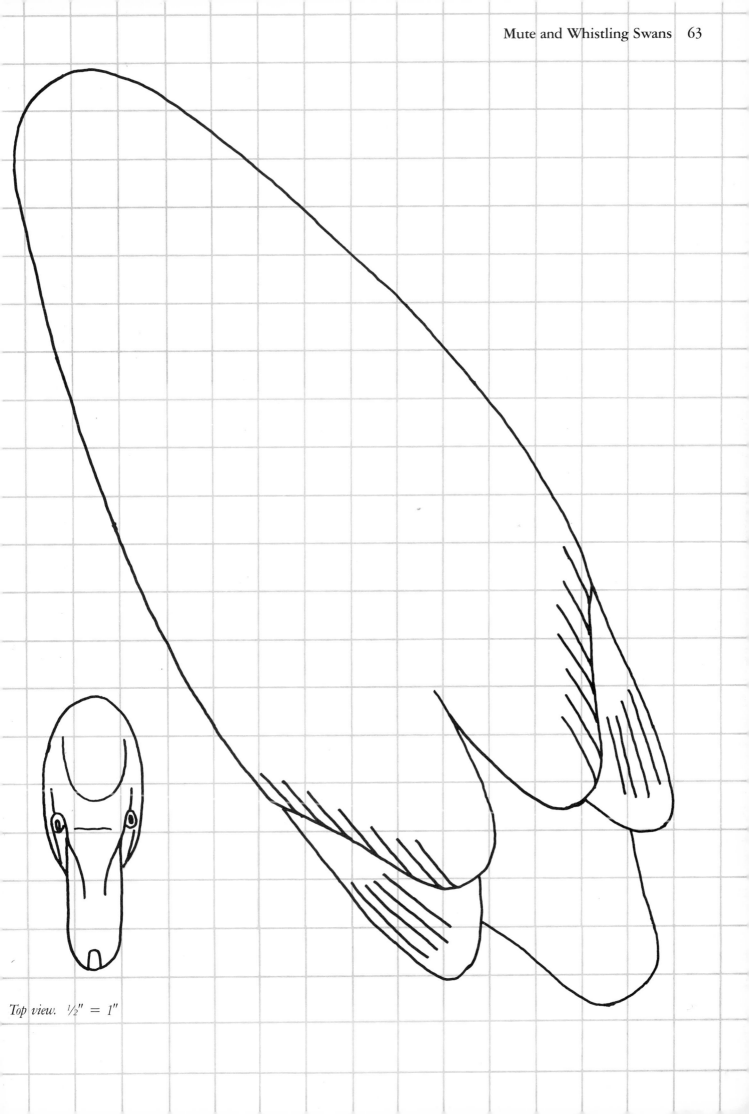

Top view. ½″ = 1″

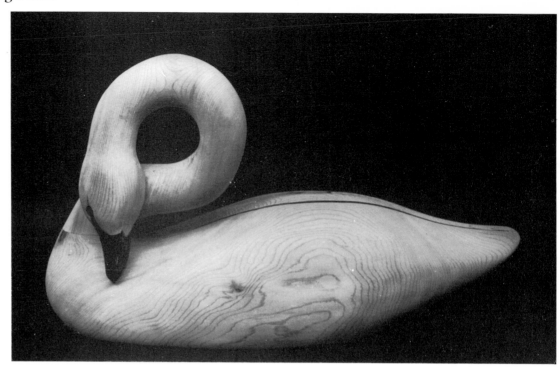

Illus. 101.   Whistling swan carved from white cedar log.

Illus. 102–103.   Head and neck views.

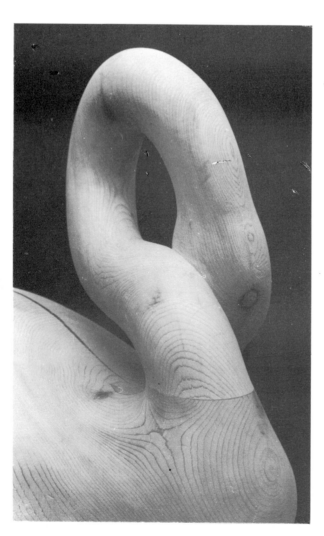 

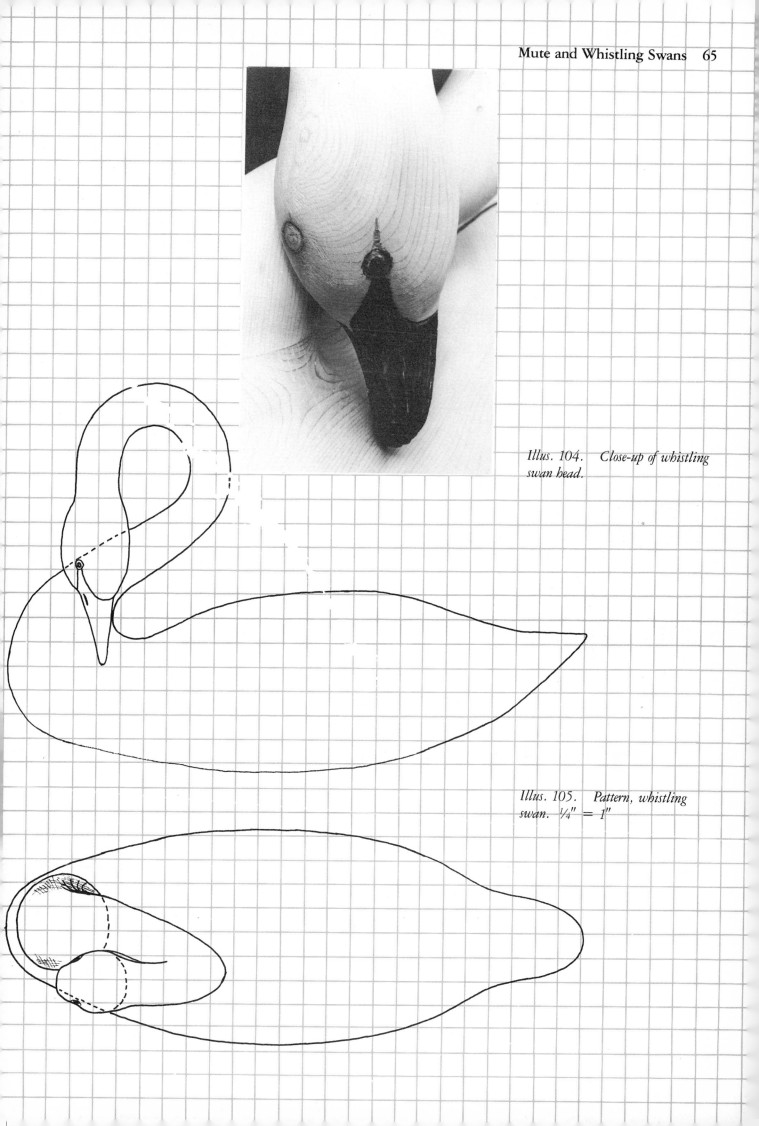

Illus. 104.   Close-up of whistling swan head.

Illus. 105.   Pattern, whistling swan. ¼" = 1"

Dwarf Penguin

Penguins are seabirds with legs located far back on their bodies. Their tails are used, along with their feet, as rudders. The wings are actually powerful flippers used in fast swimming. They are well adapted to living in and getting their food from the sea, but they can be on land for long periods of time without food. There is a big variation in size, from about sixteen inches to about forty-five or fifty inches. They can walk upright on land or ice and often slide on their bellies in snow. They are well insulated for cold climates. Penguins feed on plankton and fish. Dwarf penguins dig well-hidden holes, use natural holes in rock and earth caves or dig under rocks or plants for nests.

Illus. 106 (left).   Dwarf penguin carved from a single piece of butternut.

Illus. 107 (below left).   Side view, penguin.

Illus. 108 (below right).   Front view, penguin.

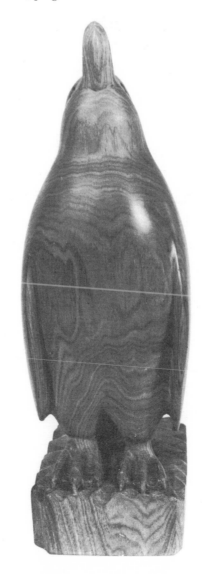

Illus. 109 (top left).   Back view, penguin.

Illus. 110 (top right).   Close-up of penguin head.

Illus. 112 (above).   Close-up of feet and tail.

Illus. 111 (left).   Close-up of penguin feet.

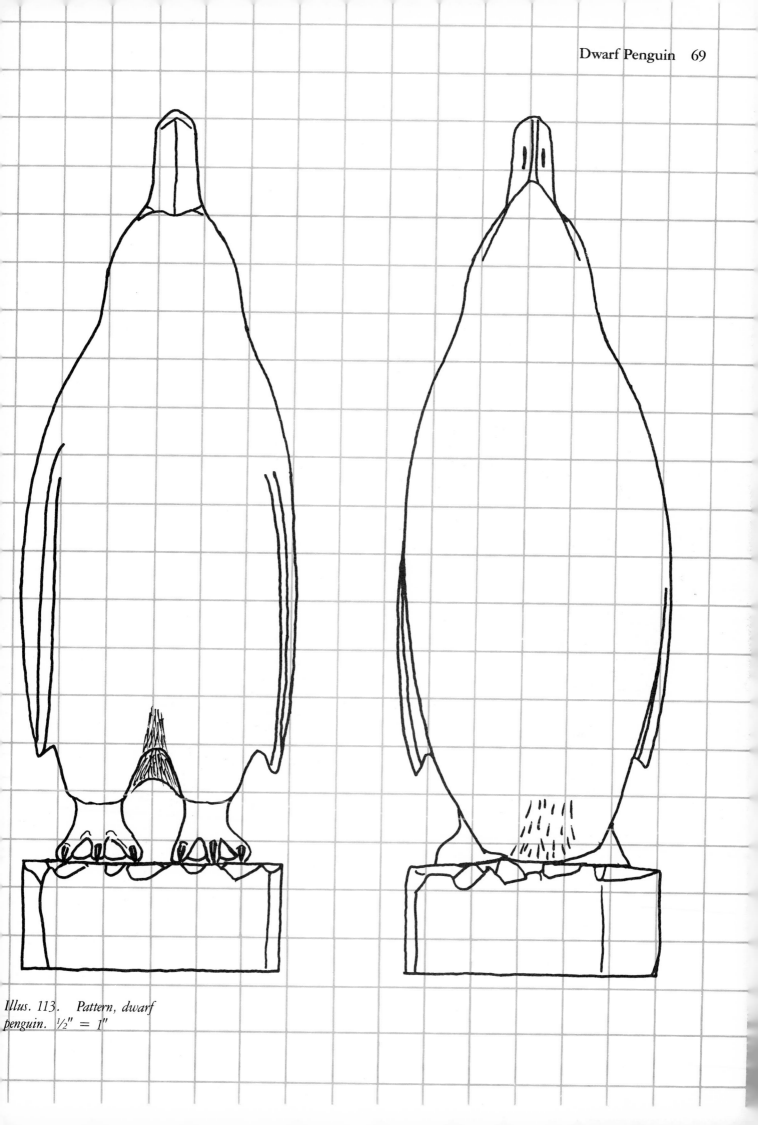

Illus. 113. Pattern, dwarf penguin. ½″ = 1″

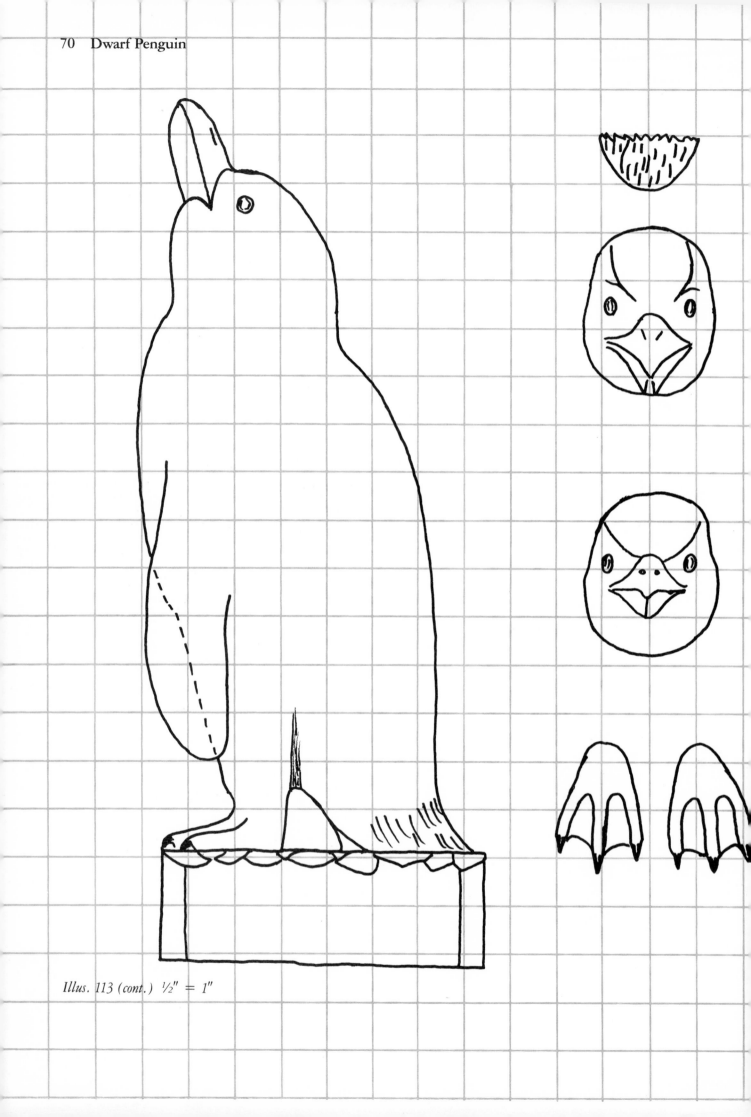

Illus. 113 *(cont.)* ½″ = 1″

Cinnamon Teal

Cinnamon teal are surface-feeding ducks, which means they do not dive as much as do the diving ducks. They live on fresh water where they get most of their food, consisting of plant matter, by dabbling. The cinnamon teal drake has a chestnut-brown nuptial plumage. The nest is often made of woven grass lined with feathers and down.

Illus. 114.   Cinnamon teal in butternut on separate base.

Illus. 115.   Top view, cinnamon teal.

Illus. 116–117.   Head and neck views.

Illus. 118.   Close-up of other details.

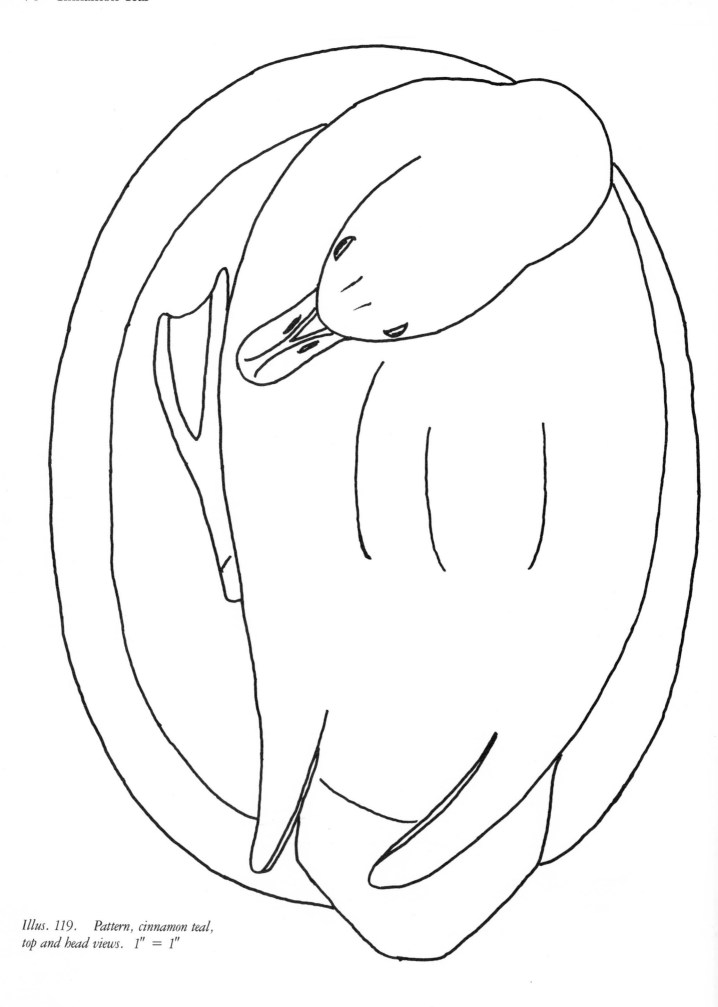

*Illus. 119. Pattern, cinnamon teal,
top and head views. 1" = 1"*

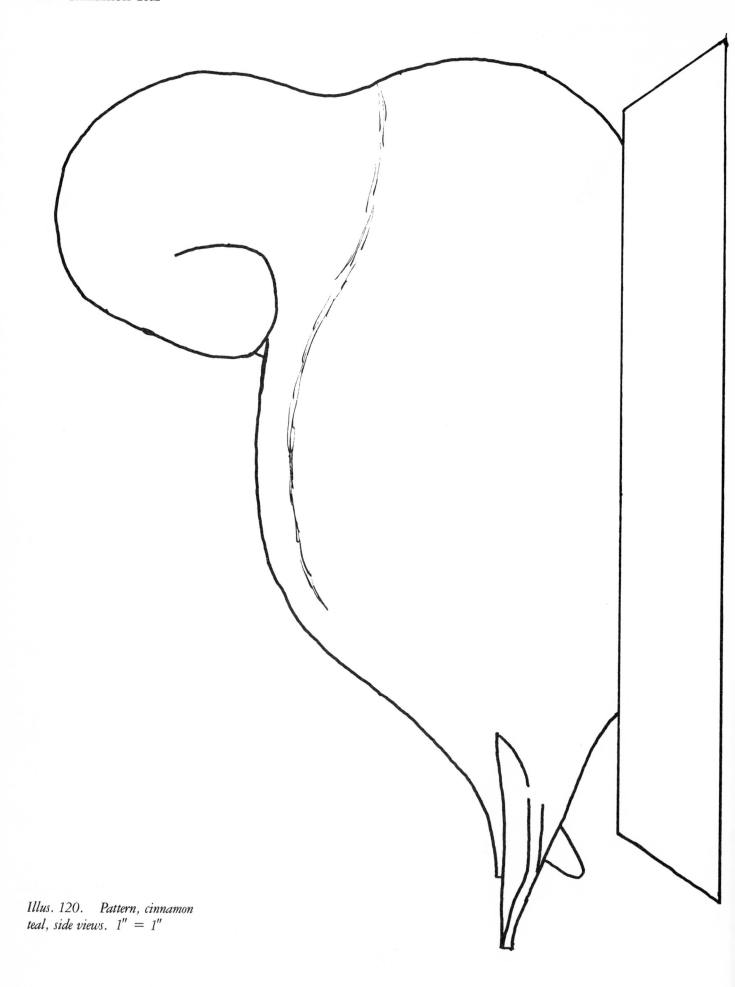

Illus. 120. Pattern, cinnamon teal, side views. 1" = 1"

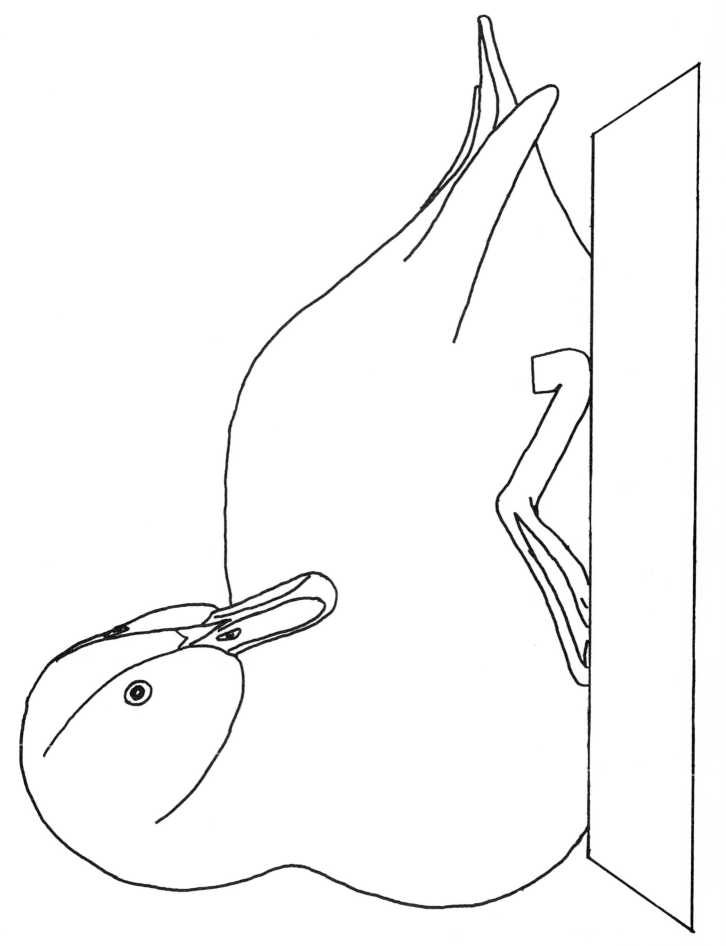

Illus. 120 (cont.)

The Brown Pelican

Brown pelicans are bulky, impressive birds with bills that may be as much as eighteen inches long. A large pouch is attached to the lower bill. The pouches are employed in catching and storing fish for their young. Sometimes they build bulky nests of sticks, or sometimes the nests are simply slightly lined hollows in the sand.

Illus. 121.   Brown pelican of laminated cedar is approximately 12" wide, 15" high, and 36" long.

Illus. 122.   Laminated members. Note head and body are laminated separately and then glued together.

Illus. 123.   Side view, rough carved.

Illus. 124.   Carving completed. Dark lines have been accented with a burning tool.

Illus. 125.   Top view of bill, completely carved.

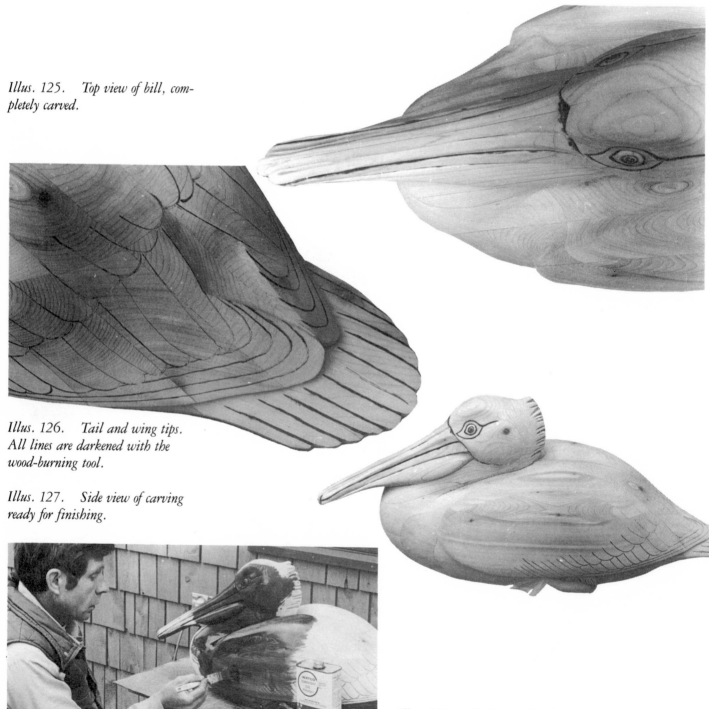

Illus. 126.   Tail and wing tips. All lines are darkened with the wood-burning tool.

Illus. 127.   Side view of carving ready for finishing.

Illus. 128.   Stain and finish is achieved with medium walnut danish oil.

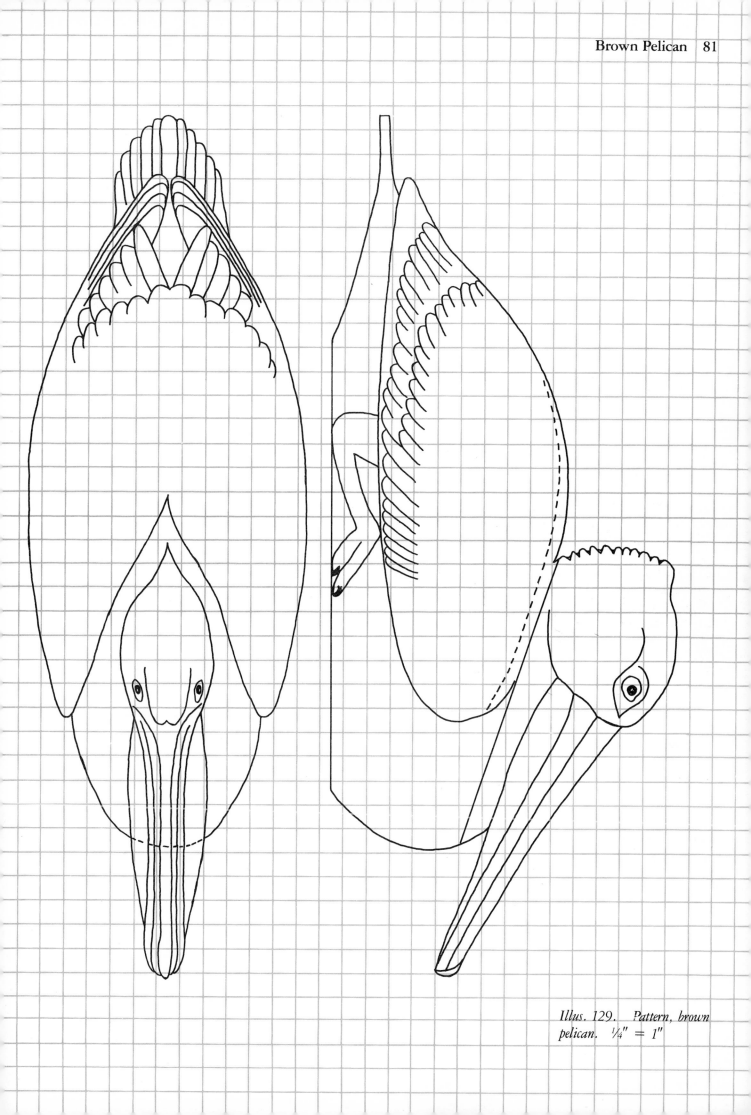

Illus. 129.   Pattern, brown pelican.   ¼" = 1"

Diurnal Birds of Prey

Birds, in general, evolved from reptilian ancestors. Birds of prey include the falcons, hawks and eagles in this book. They are not usually brightly colored. In most birds of prey, females are larger than the males. Those raptors which take live prey almost always take and kill with their toes and talons. They have acute powers of sight and full-color vision. For protection of the eyes, woods or grass birds have a third eyelid called a nictitating membrane, which is movable and transparent. A distinct feature is a bony ridge above the eye which protects the eye. Most species nest in trees, well above ground.

Duck Hawk (Peregrine Falcon)

Some prey of peregrine falcons, consist of ducks, crows, grouse, pigeons, flickers, shore birds, etc. They nest in cliff crevices and sometimes in tree cavities. They usually drop upon their prey from above.

Illus. 131.   Straight front view of duck hawk.

Illus. 130.   Duck hawk of wormy butternut on integral base.

Illus. 132–133.   Side views.

Illus. 134.   Rear view.

Illus. 135.   Head, front view.
Note *wormy texture.*

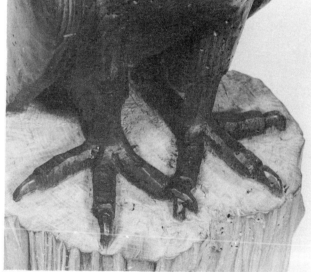

Illus. 137.   Close-up of talons.

*Illus. 136.   Head, closeup side
view.*

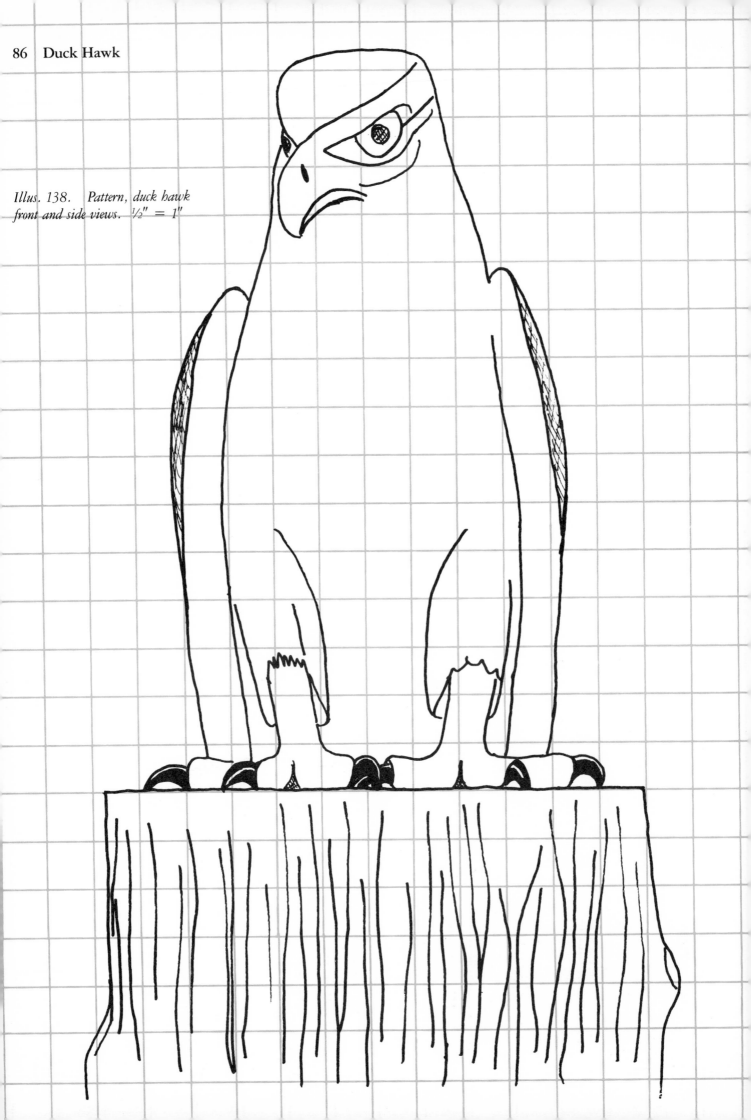

Illus. 138. Pattern, duck hawk front and side views. ½" = 1"

Illus. 138 (cont.)

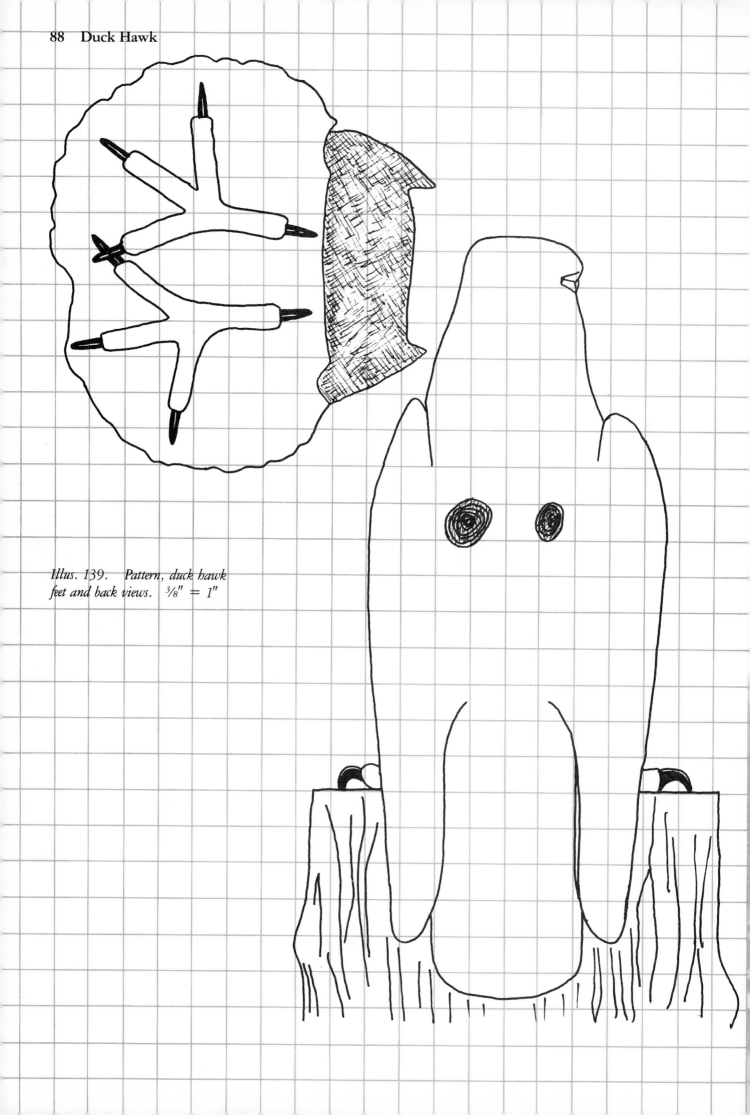

Illus. 139.   Pattern, duck hawk feet and back views.   ³⁄₈" = 1"

Sparrow Hawk or American Kestrel

They usually nest in tree cavities, rock cavities, holes in banks, or nesting boxes without nesting material. This hawk can hover with quick beats of the wing. Insects and mice form a large part of its diet.

Illus. 140.   Sparrow hawk of wormy butternut. Base and bird are one piece.

Illus. 141.   Front view of sparrow hawk.

Illus. 142.   Rear view of sparrow hawk.

Illus. 143.   Close-up, showing leg and claws of sparrow hawk.

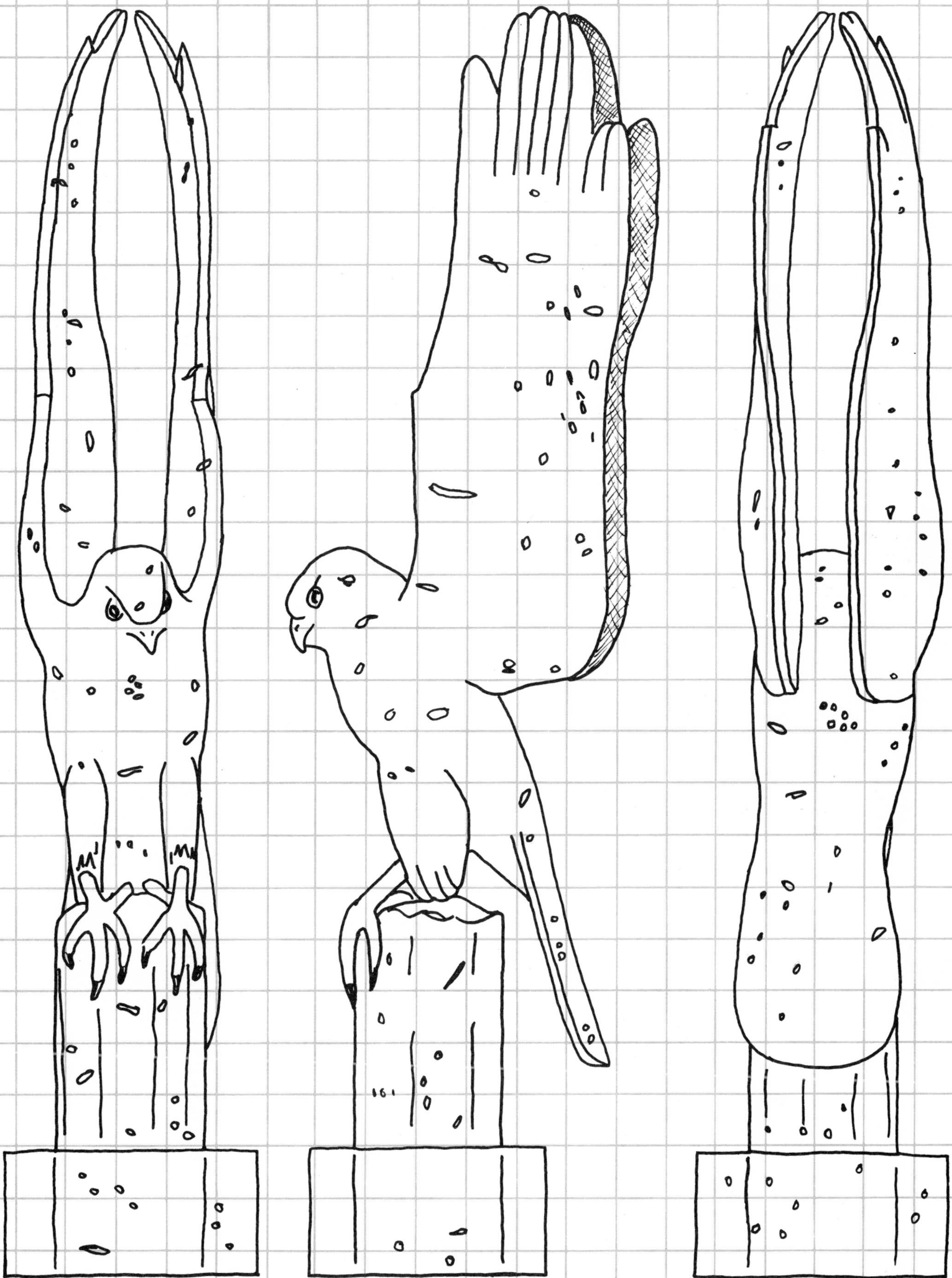

Illus. 144.   Pattern, sparrow hawk. $3/8'' = 1''$

Goshawk

Goshawks are strong hunters capable of taking prey up to the size of grouse, rabbits, and squirrels. Their nests are usually high up in evergreens, constructed of sticks, weeds, twigs, bark, grass, etc.

Illus. 145.   Goshawk carving from a single log section of wormy butternut.

Illus. 146–147.   Side views of goshawk.

Illus. 148.   Rear view of goshawk. Large crack is distinctive and interesting without weakening the carving.

Illus. 149.   Head close-up of goshawk.

Illus. 151.   Another look at the claws.

Illus. 150.   View showing claws and tail.

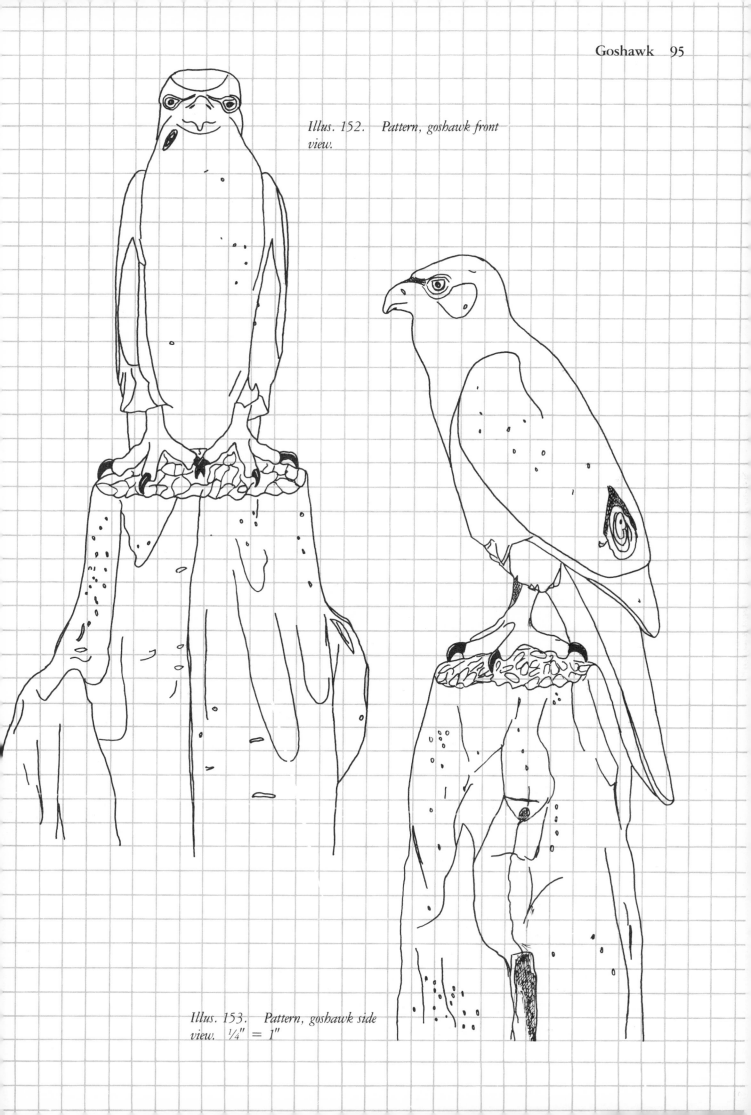

Illus. 152.   Pattern, goshawk front view.

Illus. 153.   Pattern, goshawk side view. ¼" = 1"

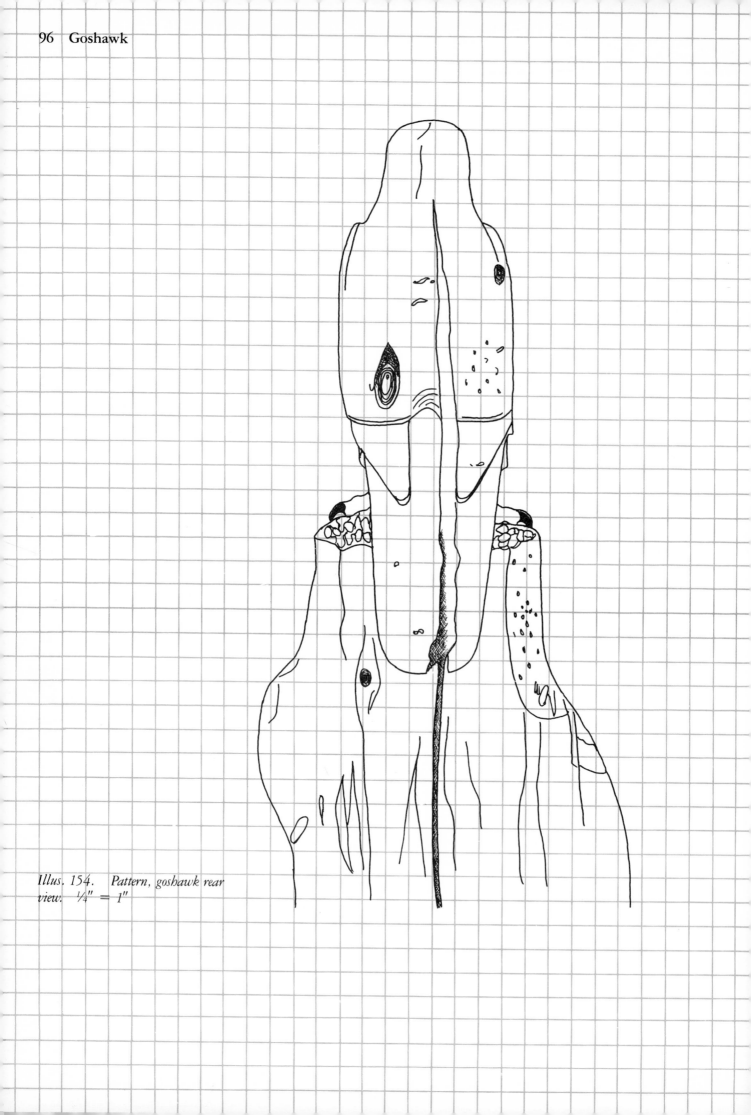

Illus. 154.   Pattern, goshawk rear view. ¼" = 1"

Broad-Winged Hawk

The broad-winged hawk's nest is usually placed in trees and constructed of sticks, roots, moss, feathers, bark, etc. Its food consists primarily of small animals, amphibians, insects, snakes, and some small birds.

Illus. 155–156.   Two views of the broad-winged hawk on one leg.

Illus. 156.   Base and bird are carved from the same, rugged timber.

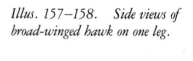

Illus. 157–158.   Side views of broad-winged hawk on one leg.

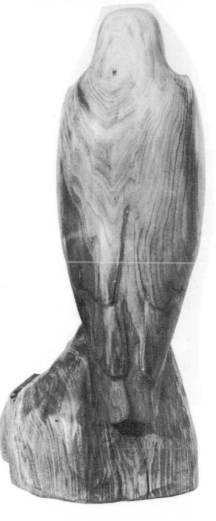

Illus. 159.   Rear view.

Illus. 160.   Leg detail. Note second leg above in folded position.

Illus. 161.   Front view close-up of head.

Illus. 162.   Head close-up. Beak surfaces have been woodburned.

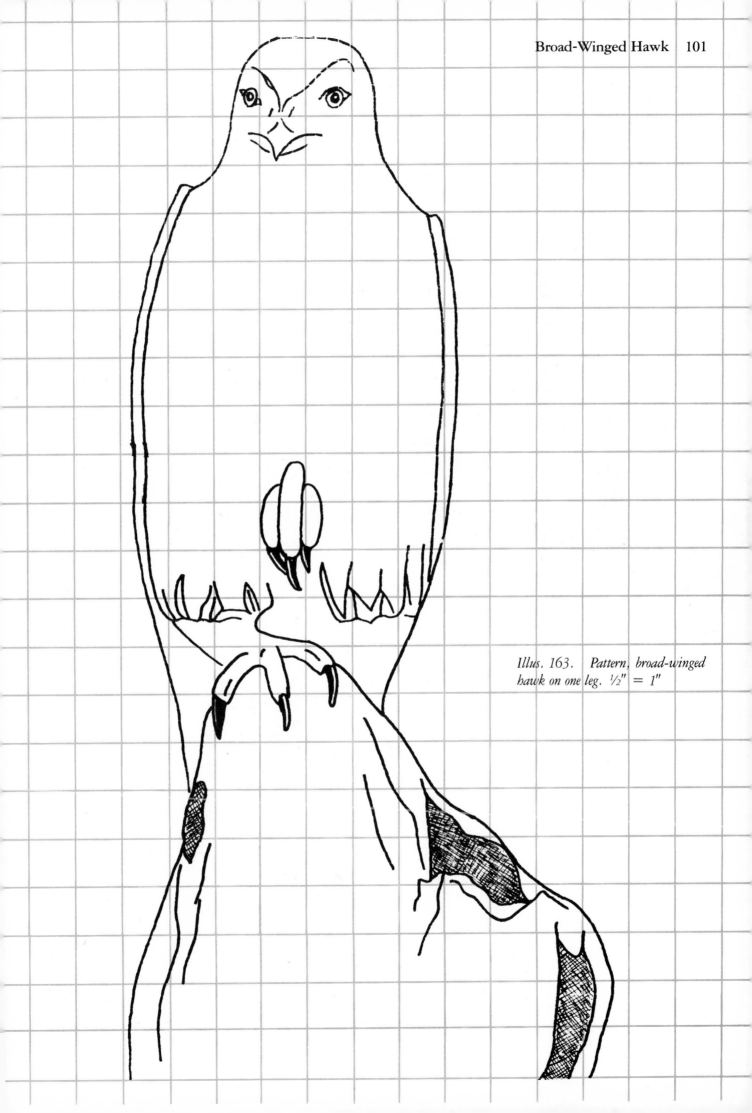

Illus. 163.   Pattern, broad-winged hawk on one leg. ½" = 1"

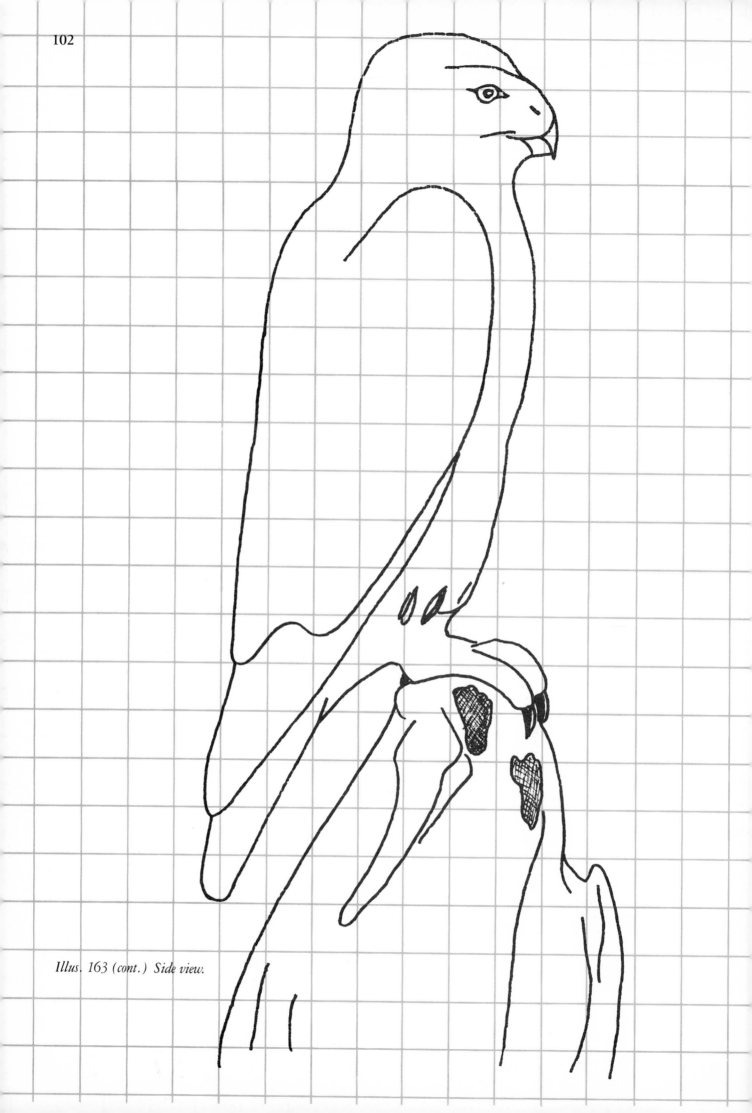

Illus. 163 (cont.) Side view.

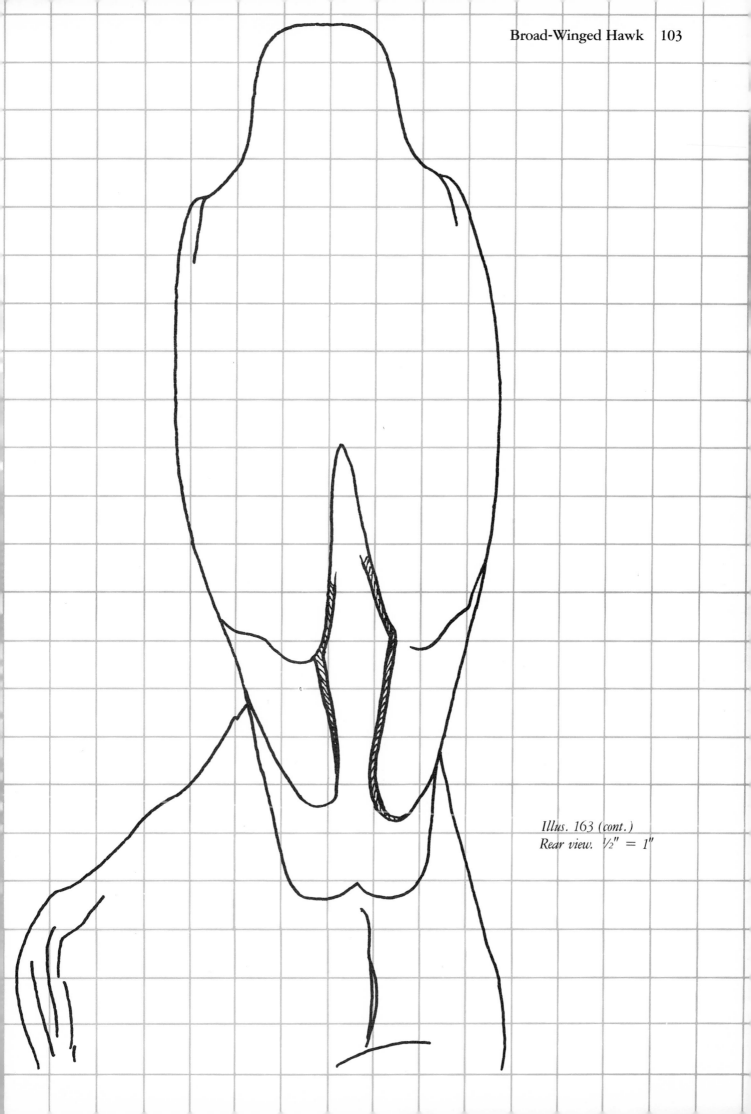

Illus. 163 (cont.)
Rear view. ½" = 1"

*Illus. 164.   Broad-winged hawk
carved on a black ash crotch.*

Illus. 165.   Front view.

Illus. 166.   Side view.

Illus. 167.   Note the part of this base formed by nature compared to the branch end shaped by man shown in Illus. 170.

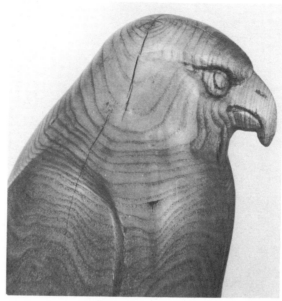

Illus. 168.   Head close-up.

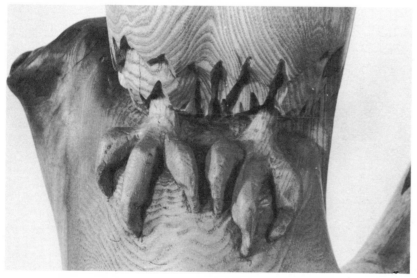

Illus. 169.   Talons of the ash broad-winged hawk.

Illus. 170.   Branch end is hollowed and shaped with chain saw.

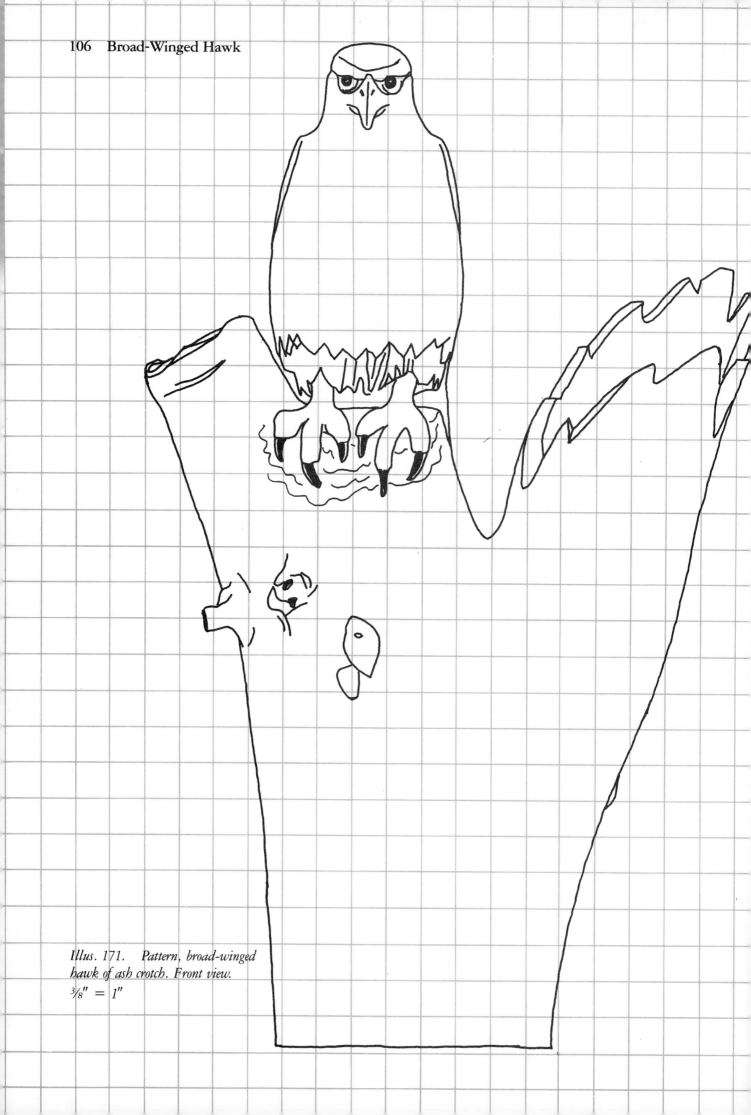

*Illus. 171.   Pattern, broad-winged
hawk of ash crotch. Front view.*
$\frac{3}{8}'' = 1''$

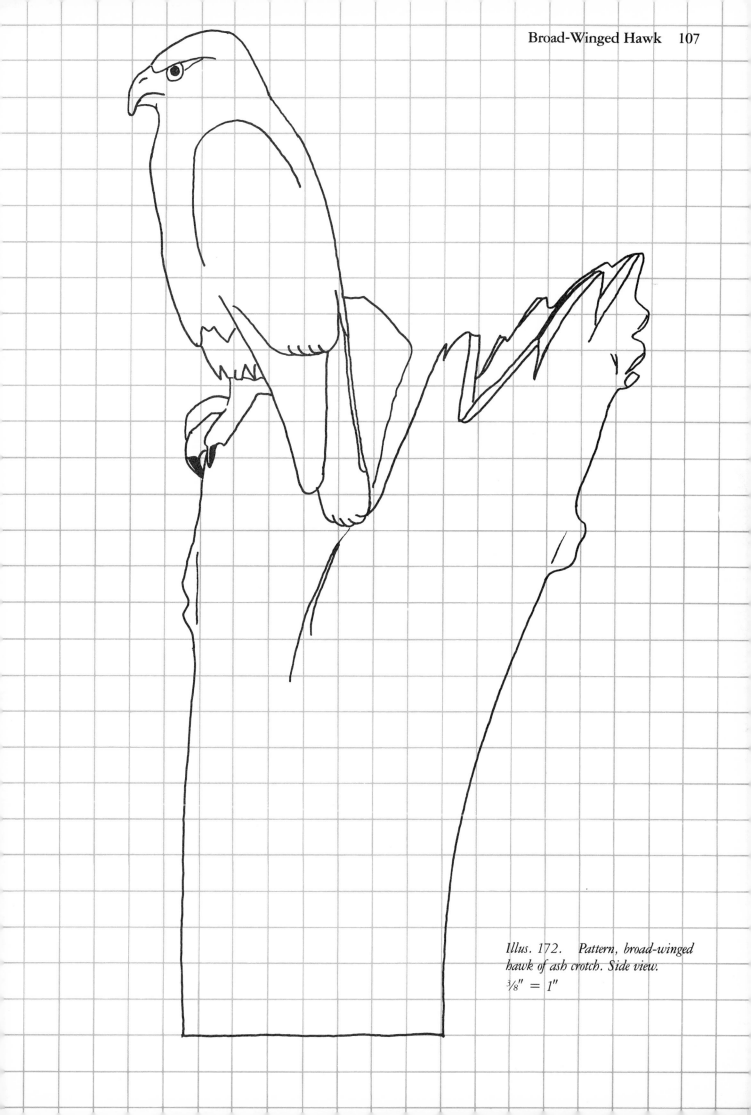

Illus. 172.   Pattern, broad-winged hawk of ash crotch. Side view.
⅜″ = 1″

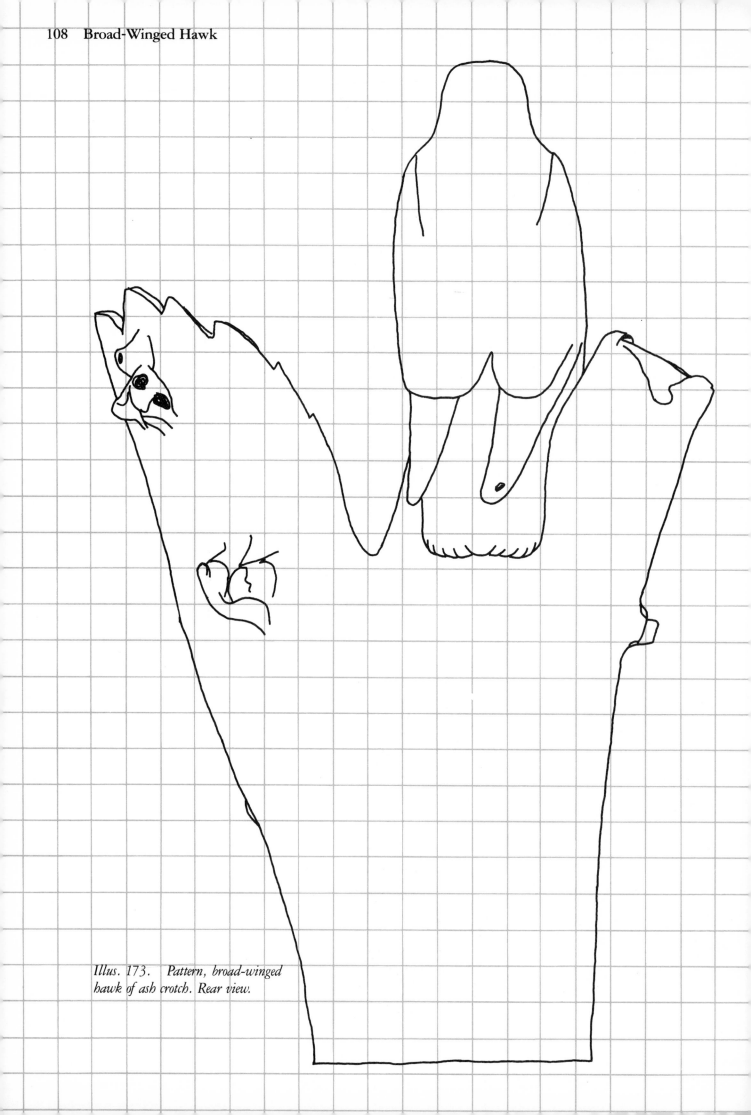

Illus. 173.   Pattern, broad-winged hawk of ash crotch. Rear view.

Illus. 174. Walnut broad-winged hawk with rat.

Illus. 175–176. Side views of hawk with rat.

Illus. 177. Rear view.

Illus. 178–180.   Views of the rough carving.

Illus. 181.   Bark will be removed.

Illus. 182.   One closeup look at the carved rat.

Illus. 183.   Another look at the carved rat. Notice the carved knot-hole.

Illus. 184.   Close-up of hawk head.

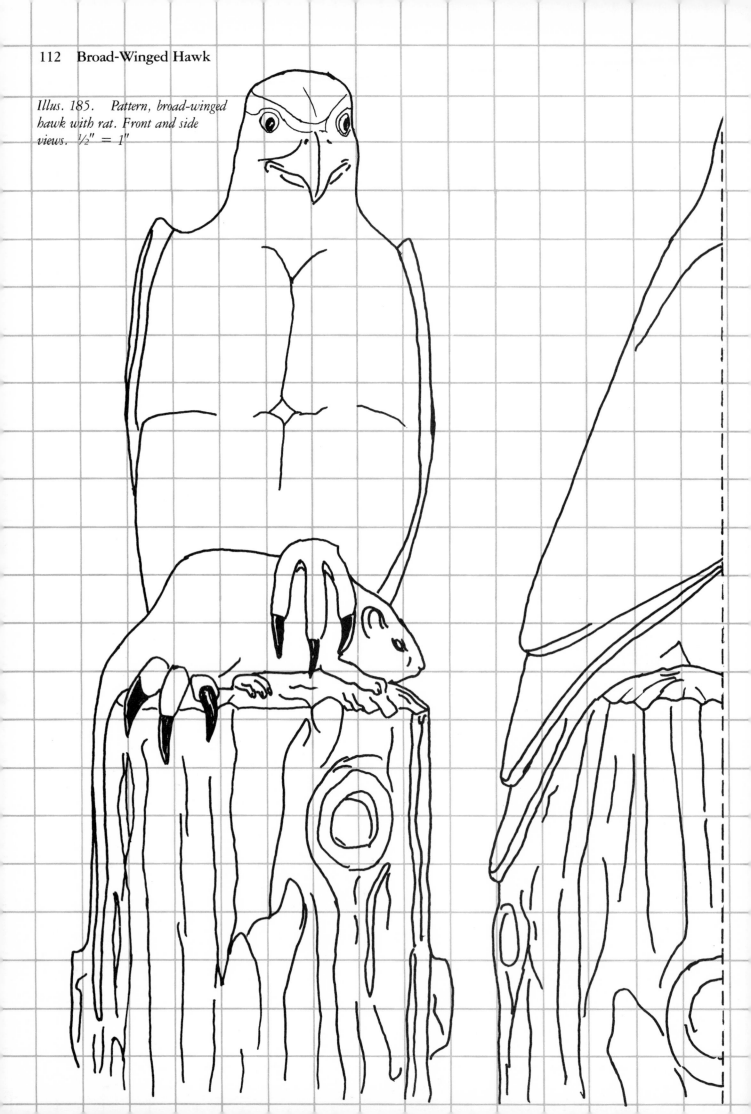

Illus. 185.   Pattern, broad-winged hawk with rat. Front and side views. ½" = 1"

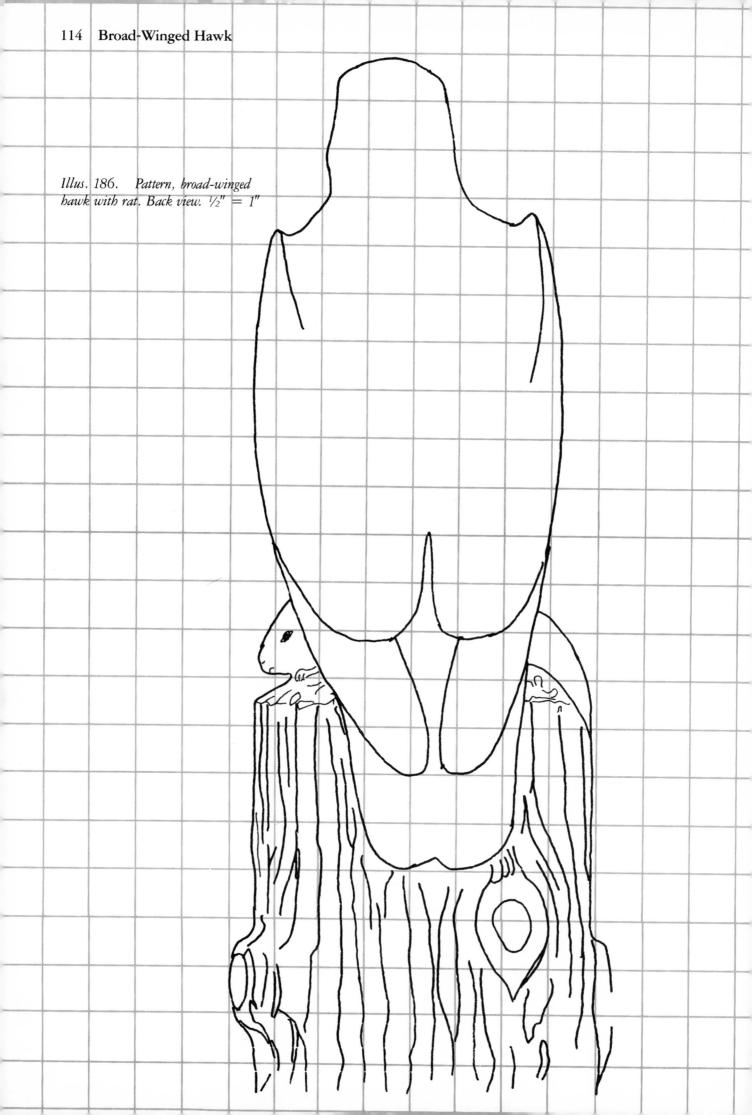

Illus. 186.   Pattern, broad-winged hawk with rat. Back view. ½" = 1"

Owls

Owls have large heads, eyes directed forward for good binocular vision. Their soft plumage helps them in silent flight. Most are nocturnal birds and capture their prey with their feet. They have sensitive eyesight and hearing. The feather tufts on the head of some owls are not ears but adornment. The ears lie beneath the facial disk and face forward. Owls are chiefly rodent eaters, along with a few small mammals, reptiles, amphibians, insects and birds. They may nest in large trees with natural cavities or in old nests made and deserted by hawks, crows, or squirrels. Owls have two toes pointing forward and two backward.

Great Horned Owl

These owls are horned or tufted. Very large owls, they are capable of preying on animals such as rabbits, game birds, even an occasional skunk. They nest in nests made and deserted by other large birds, or in caves and hollow trees.

Illus. 187.   Great horned owl carved into a cedar log.

Illus. 188.   First, lay out size.

Illus. 189.   Make rough layout with felt marker.

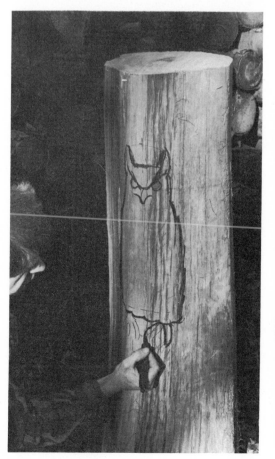

Illus. 190.   Make vertical roughing cuts as shown.

 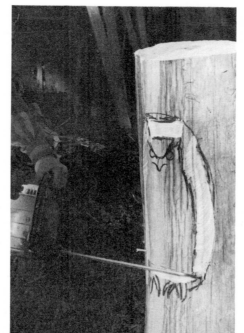 

Illus. 191–193.   With tip of chain saw, make horizontal roughing cuts.

Illus. 194 (above).   Deepen side openings.

Illus. 195 (top right).   Closeup look at the head. All lines and markings are emphasized with a wood-burning tool.

Illus. 196 (right).   Claw surfaces are woodburned as are the bar markings of the body.

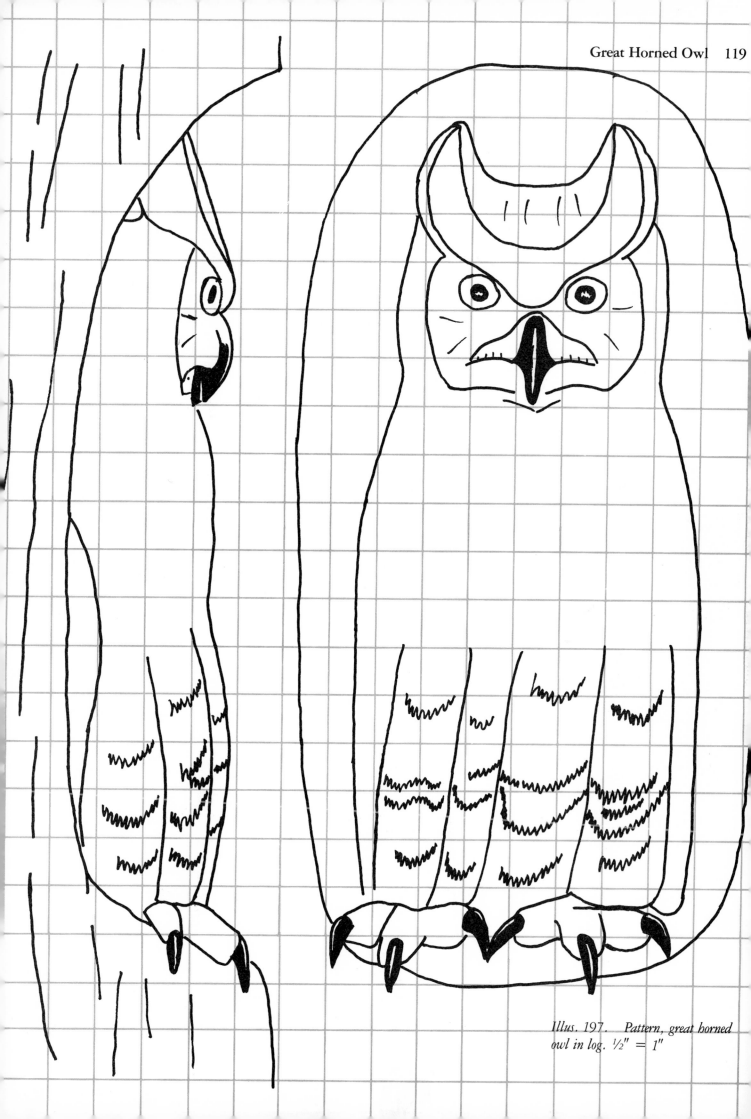

Illus. 197.   Pattern, great horned owl in log. ½" = 1"

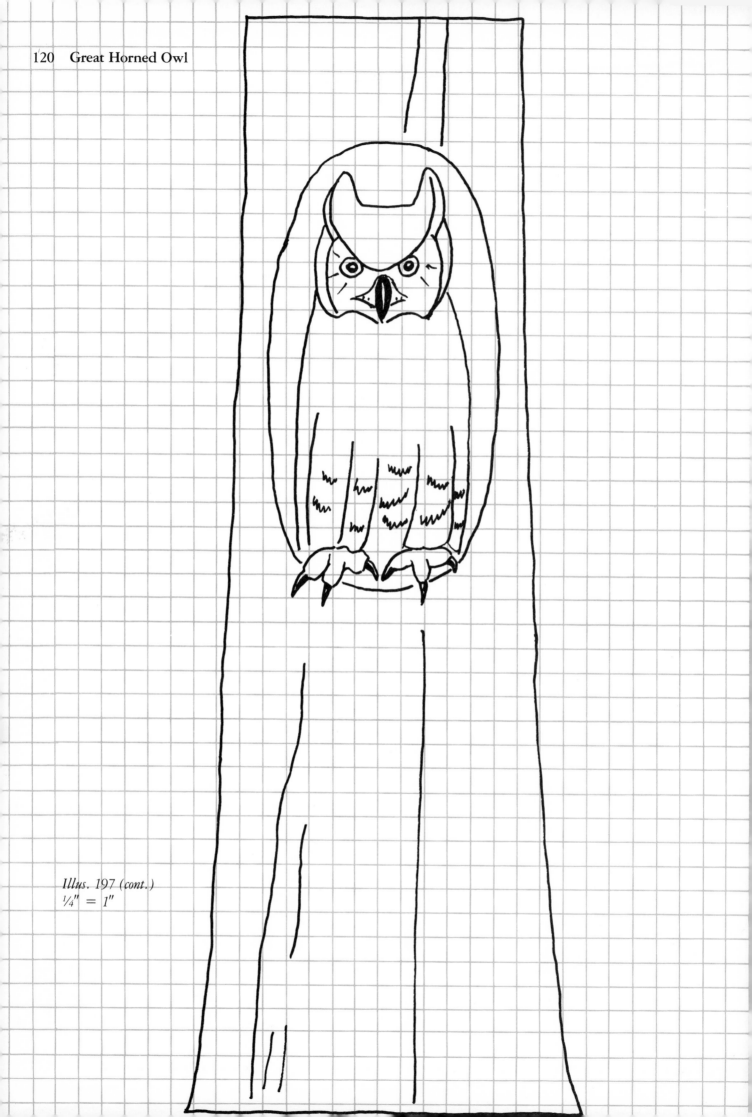

Illus. 197 (cont.)
$\frac{1}{4}'' = 1''$

Illus. 198. *Great horned owl in butternut. This carving is all from one piece of wood, but designed to look like 2 or 3 individual pieces.*

Illus. 199. *Side view of great horned owl.*

Illus. 200. *Rear view.*

Illus. 201. Closeup view of great horned owl head.

Illus. 202. Side view of claws,

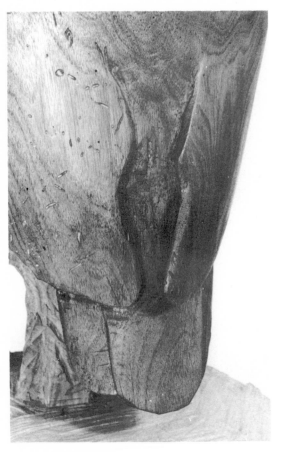

Illus. 203. Feet and claws grasping the carved perch.

Illus. 204. Rear tail detail.

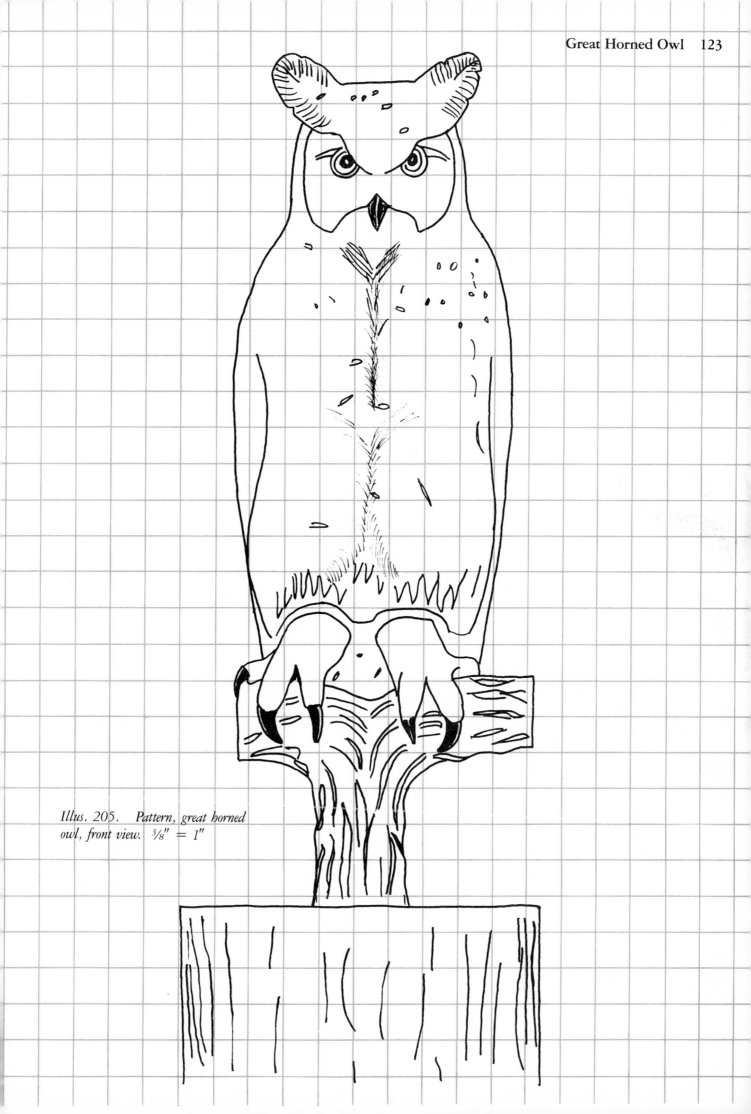

Illus. 205.   Pattern, great horned owl, front view. ⅜″ = 1″

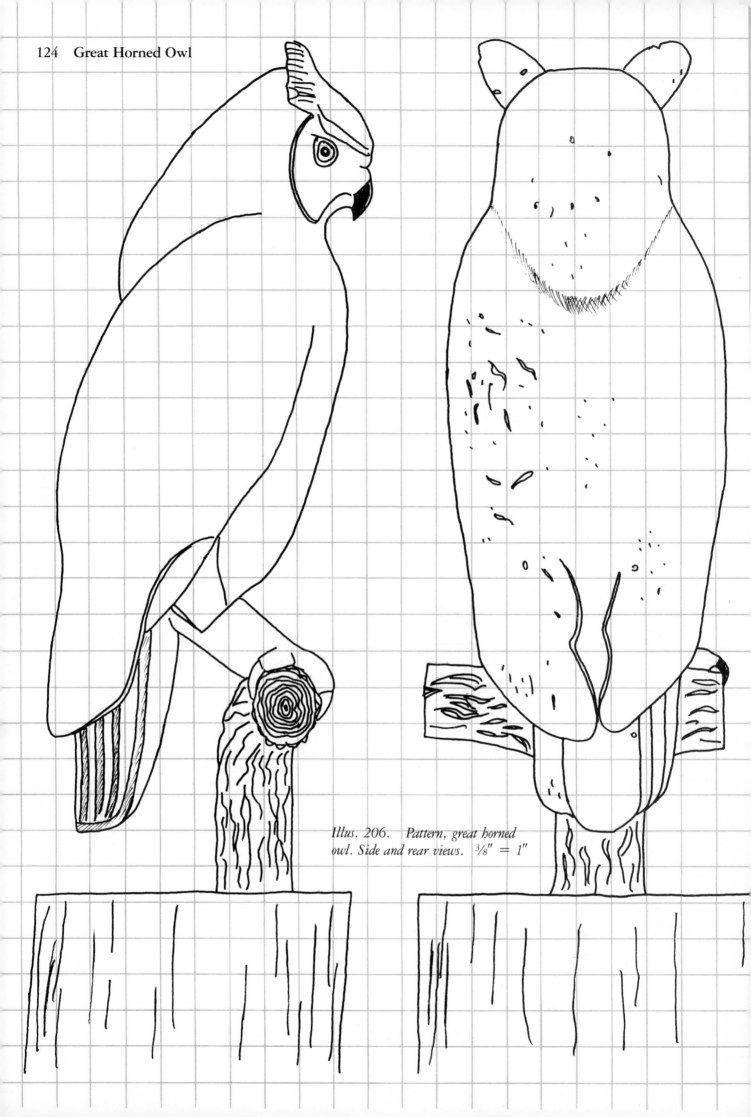

Illus. 206. Pattern, great horned owl. Side and rear views. ³⁄₈" = 1"

Illus. 207.   Great horned owl with rabbit. Carved from box elder crotch.

Illus. 208–209.   Side views of great horned owl with a rabbit.

Illus. 211–212.   Roughing out with the chain saw.

Illus. 210.   Rear view.

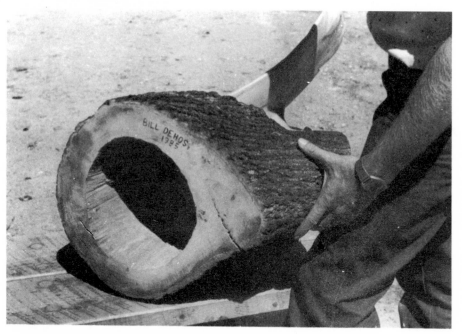

Illus. 213.   Base is hollowed with chain saw to minimize cracking stresses and lighten carving.

Illus. 214.   Starting to rough-carve with the gouge.

Illus. 215–216.   Further shaping with gouge starts to reveal detail.

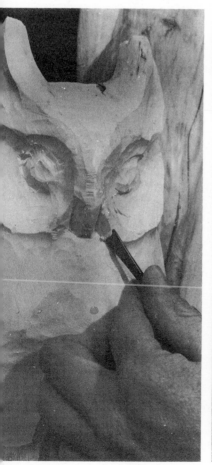
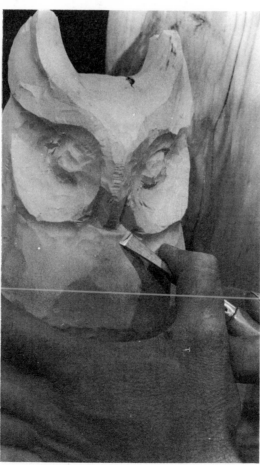
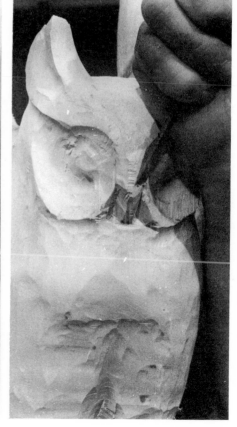

Illus. 217–219.   Working the bill area with flat carving chisel.

Illus. 220.   Emphasize claw by
undercutting with small gouge.

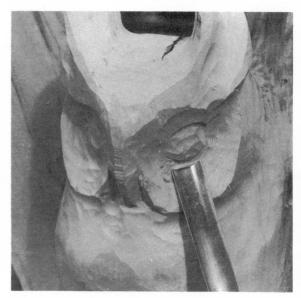

Illus. 221.   Carving the eye area
with a gouge.

Illus. 222.   Carving rabbit's foot
with a v-parting tool.

Illus. 223.   Separating the rabbit
and base with a v-parting tool.

Illus. 224.   Carving the rabbit's
eye with small v-parting tool.

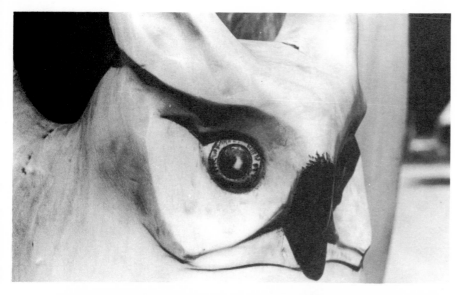

Illus. 225.   Close-up of completed head with woodburned eye and bill.

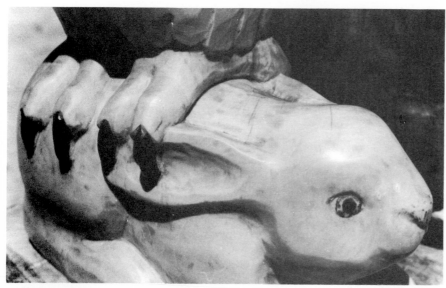

Illus. 226.   Close-up of owl's feet and rabbit detail. Note *the natural, lustre of the raw box elder wood.*

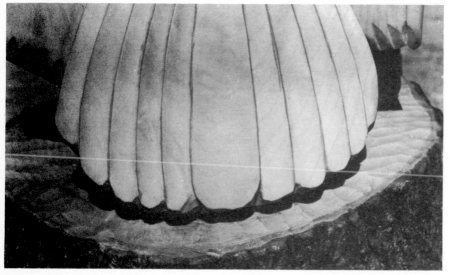

Illus. 227.   Rear-tail detail.

Illus. 228.   Wing-tip detail.

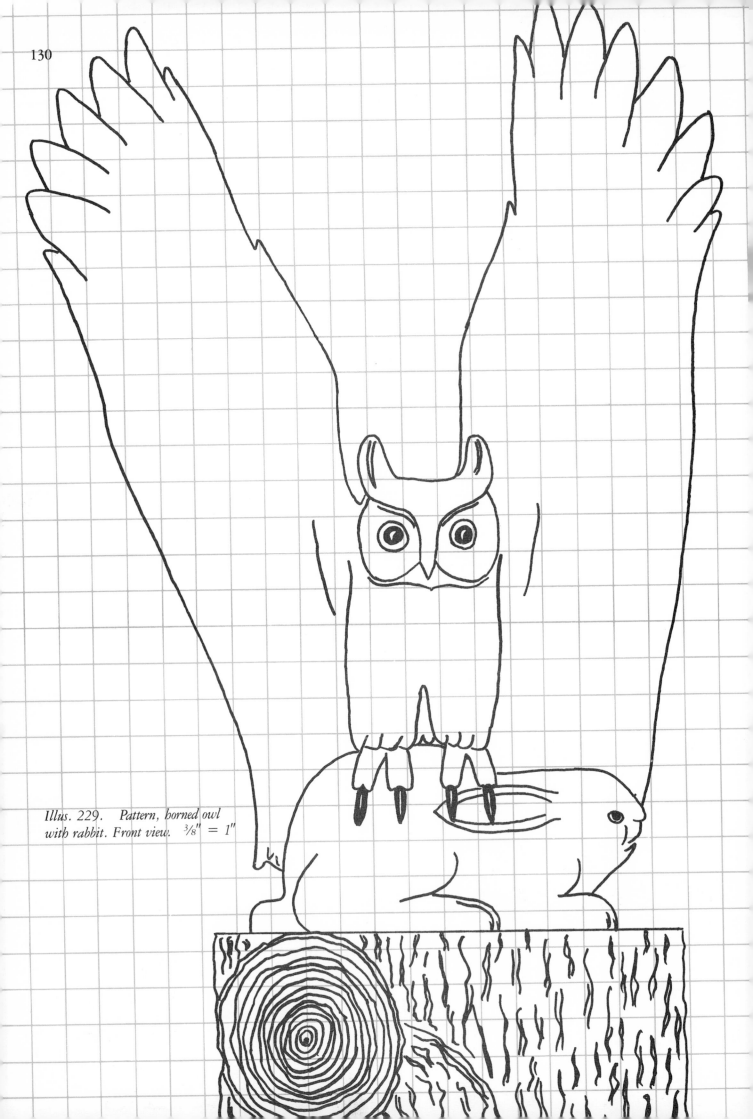

130

*Illus. 229.   Pattern, horned owl
with rabbit. Front view. $^3/_8'' = 1''$*

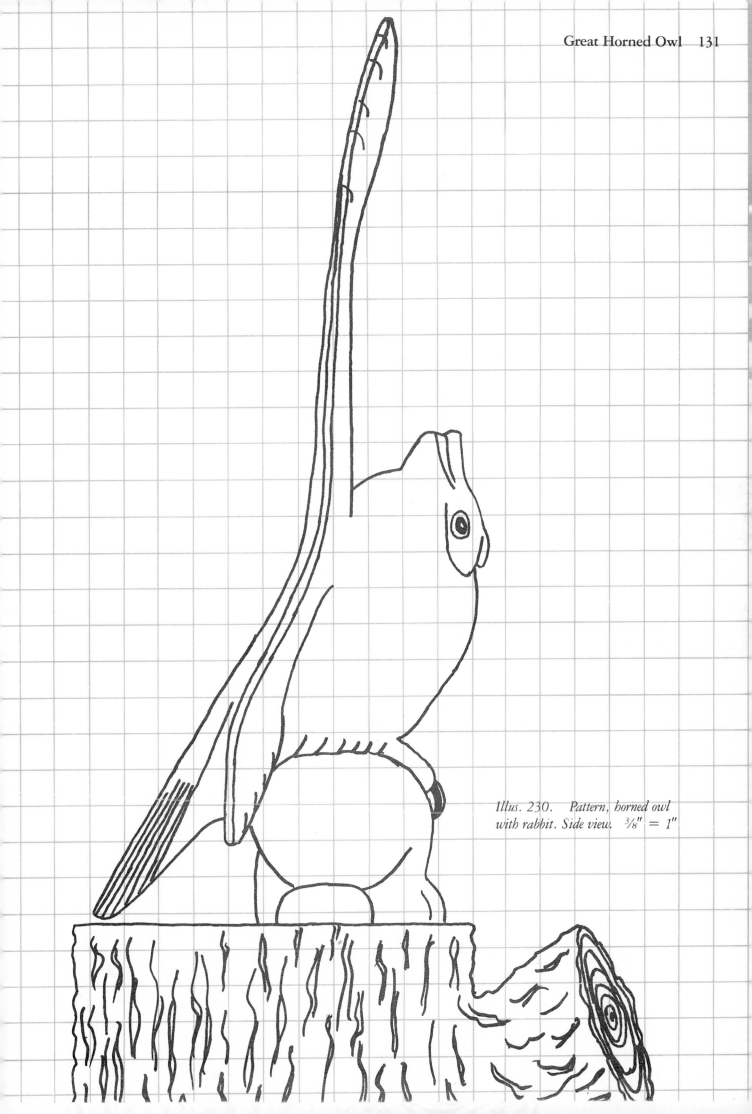

Illus. 230.   Pattern, horned owl with rabbit. Side view. ³⁄₈″ = 1″

Illus. 231.   Pattern, great horned owl with rabbit. Side view. ³⁄₈" = 1"

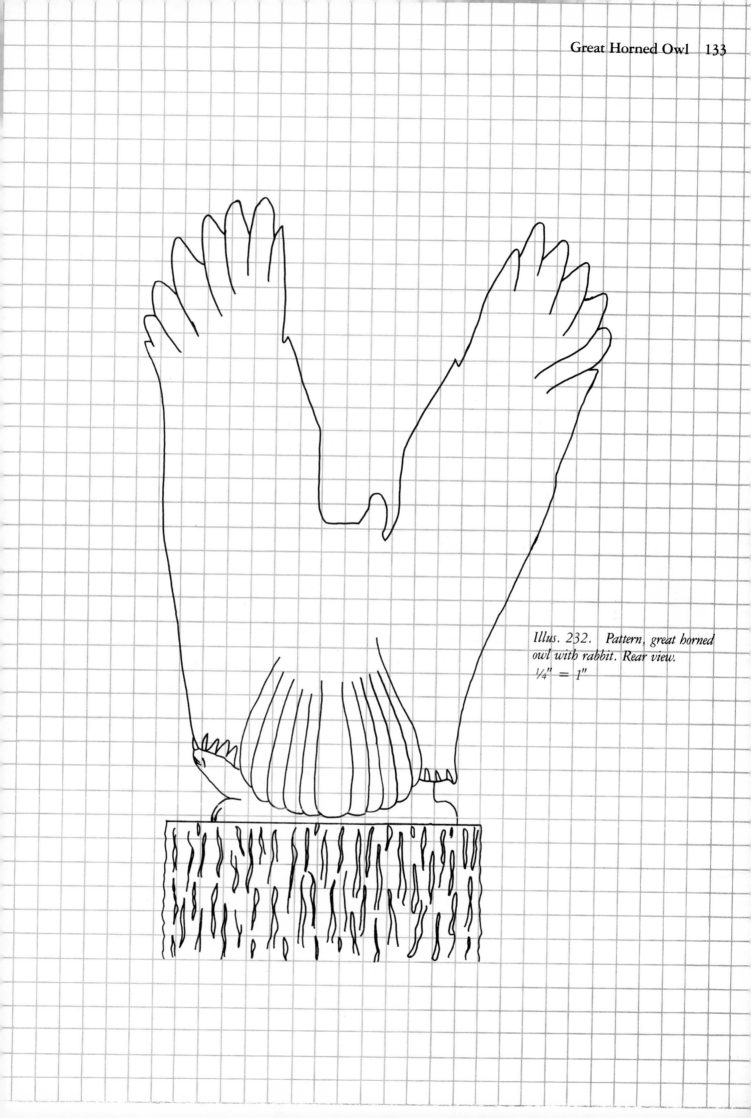

Illus. 232.   Pattern, great horned owl with rabbit. Rear view.
¼" = 1"

Illus. 233.   Great horned owl, butternut, one-piece crotch, clutching a red squirrel. This carving measures 32" wide and 38" high.

Illus. 234.   Another view.

Illus. 236–237.   Close-up views of claws and squirrel. Note undercutting of the talons.

Illus. 235.   Head close-up of great horned owl.

Illus. 238.   Pattern, great horned owl with red squirrel. Front view.
¼" = 1"

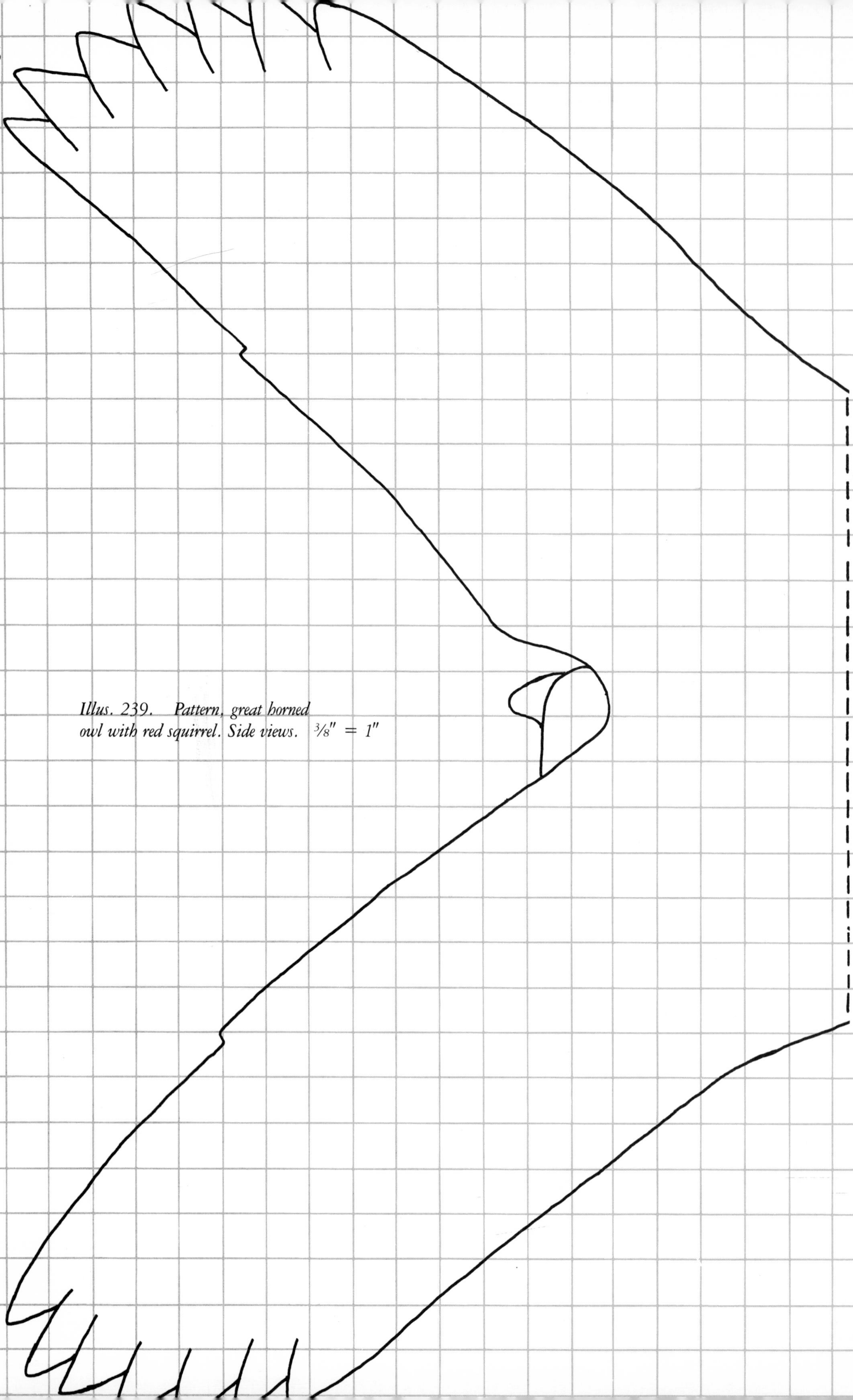

136

Illus. 239.   Pattern, great horned
owl with red squirrel. Side views. $^3/_8'' = 1''$

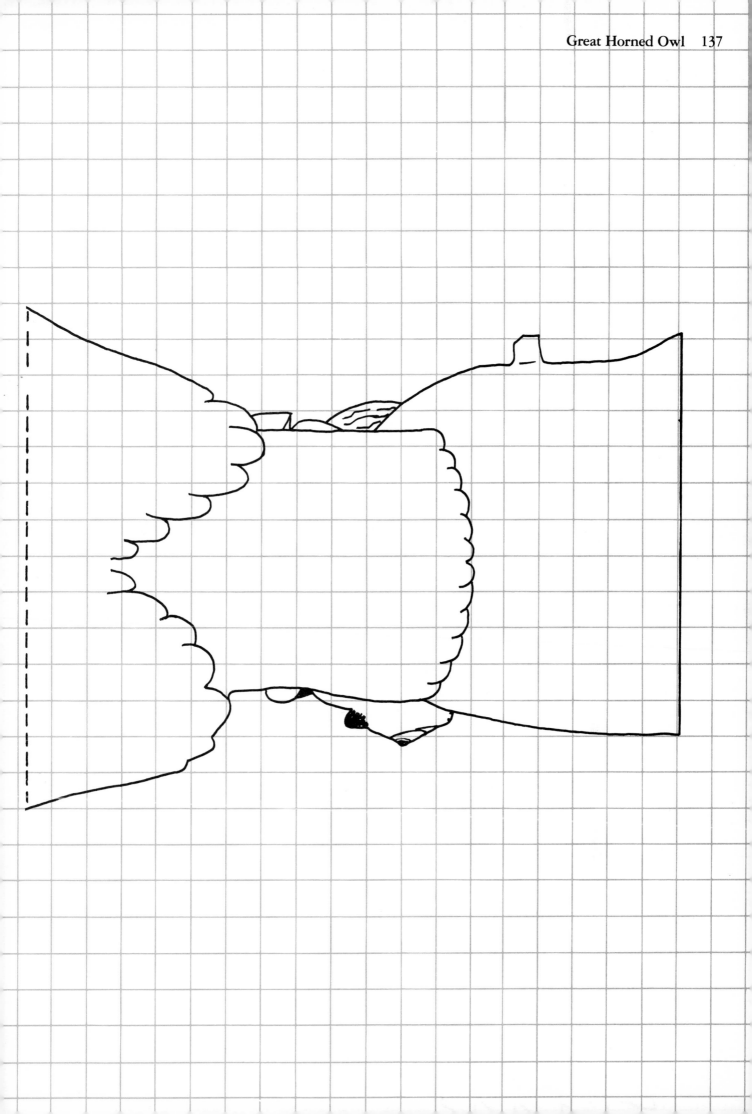

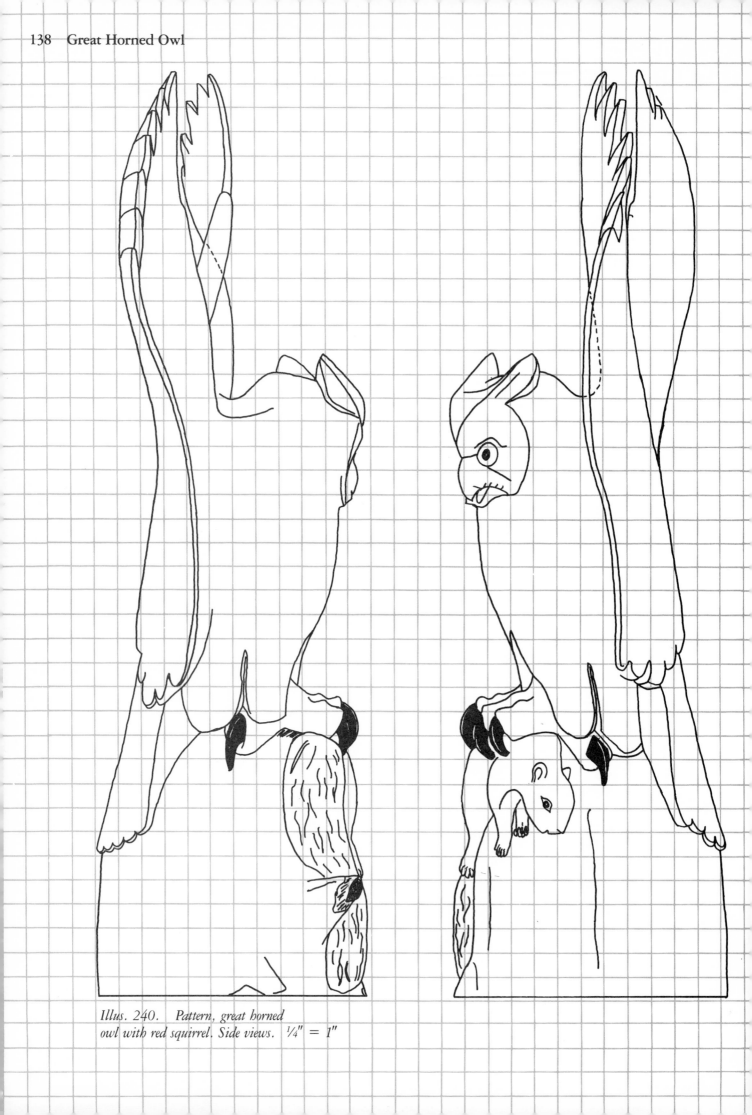

Illus. 240.   Pattern, great horned
owl with red squirrel. Side views.   ¼" = 1"

Barn Owl (Monkey-Faced Owl)

Barn owls seek protection in old buildings, tree cavities, caves, etc. The facial veil is somewhat heart-shaped with black-brown eyes. The barn owl hunts in open country. It catches small mammals up to the size of rats and also small birds.

*Illus. 241.   Barn owl with
field mouse in wormy butternut.*

*Illus. 242.   Front view. Note
this carving is made from one piece
of stock that's been carved to look
like it's made in two pieces.*

Illus. 243–244.   Side views.

Illus. 245. Rear view.

Illus. 246. Head close-up of the barn owl.

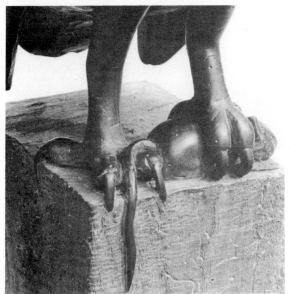

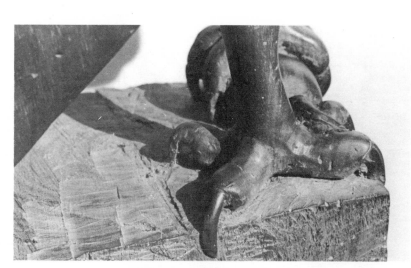

Illus. 247–250. Various views of feet, claw, mouse, and base details.

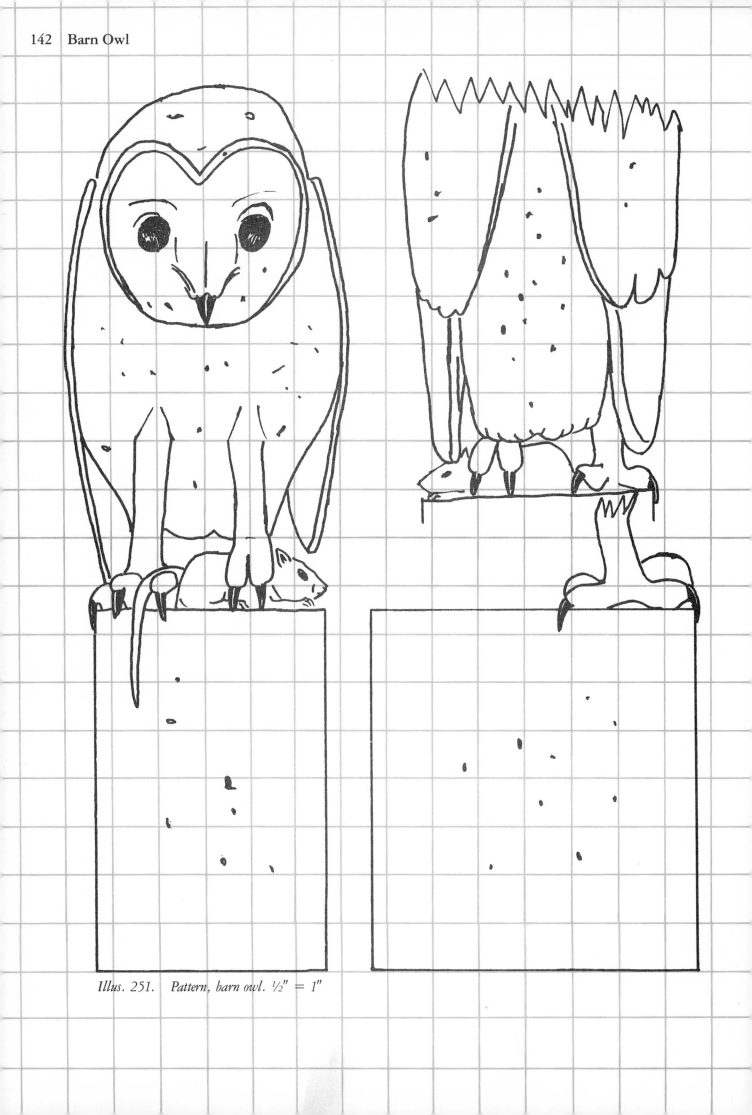

Illus. 251.   Pattern, barn owl. ½" = 1"

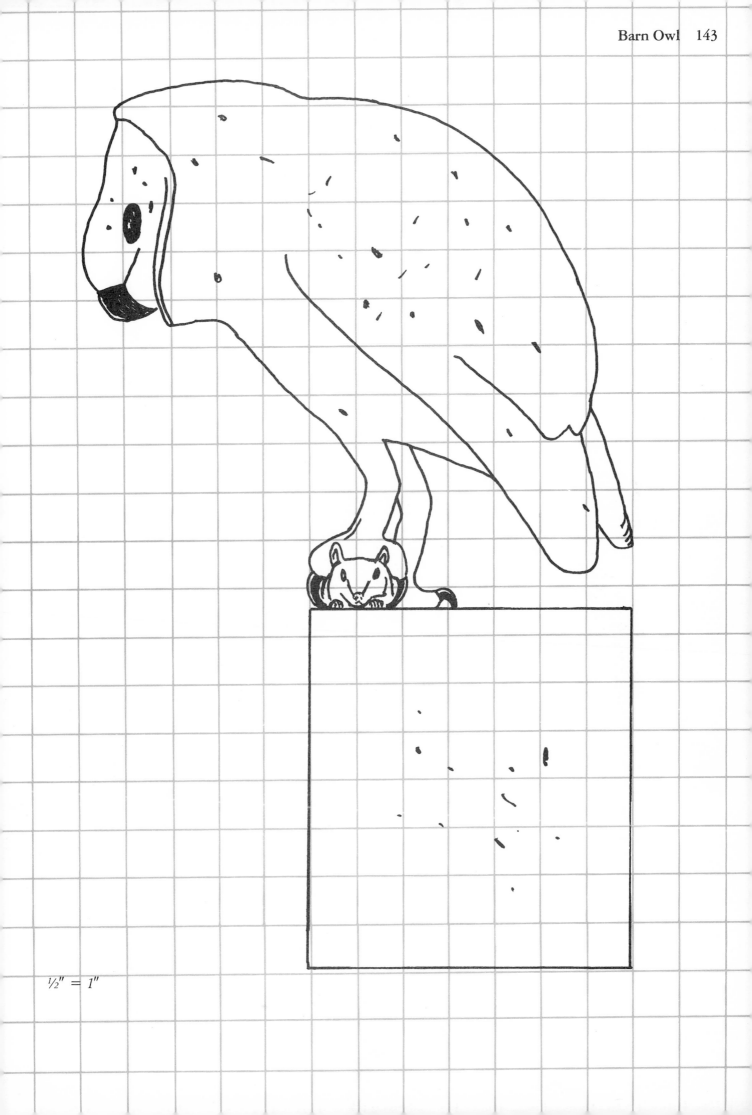

½″ = 1″

Barred Owl (Hoot Owl)

Barred owls' heads are basically round with no ear tufts and brown eyes. Woodland owls, they like the thick woods and swamps. Their calls are very impressive. Food consists of small animals and small birds, etc.

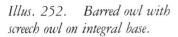
Illus. 252.   Barred owl with screech owl on integral base.

Illus. 253.   Front view of barred owl. Note: *Screech owl (head only visible) is upside down.*

Illus. 254–255.   Side views. Note: *Base is left natural and unfinished for contrast.*

Illus. 257.   Head close-up of the barred owl.

Illus. 256.   Rear view.

Illus. 258.   Closeup look at the "upside-down" head of the screech owl.

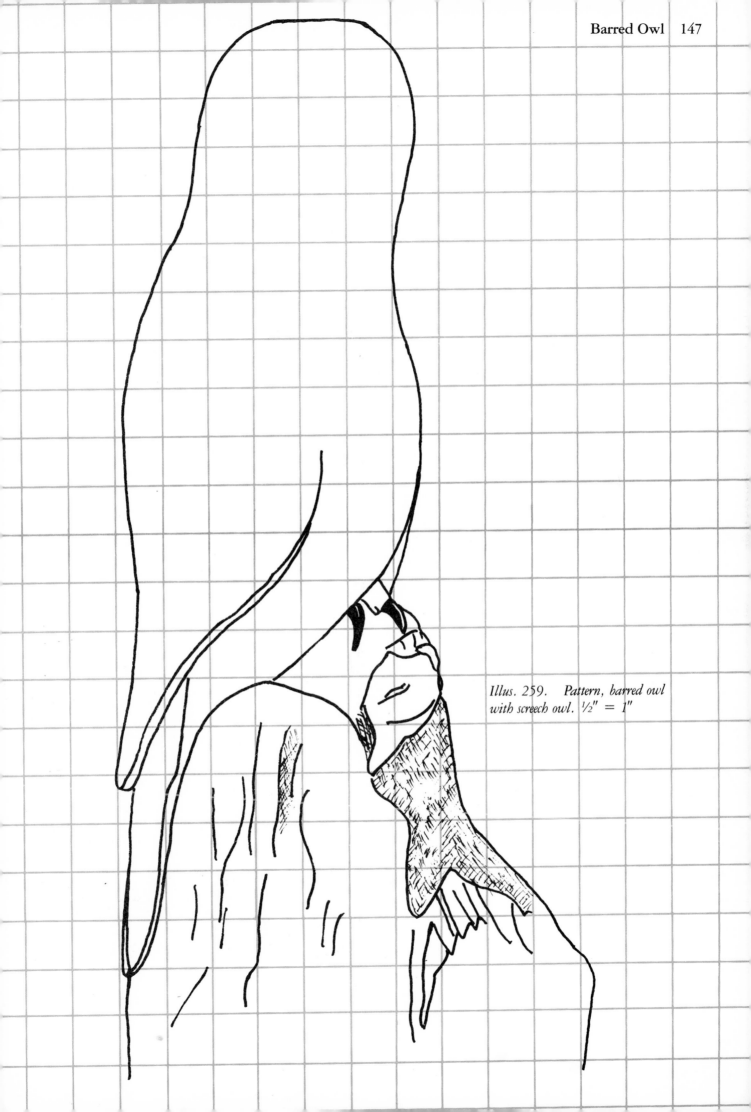

Illus. 259. Pattern, barred owl with screech owl. ½" = 1"

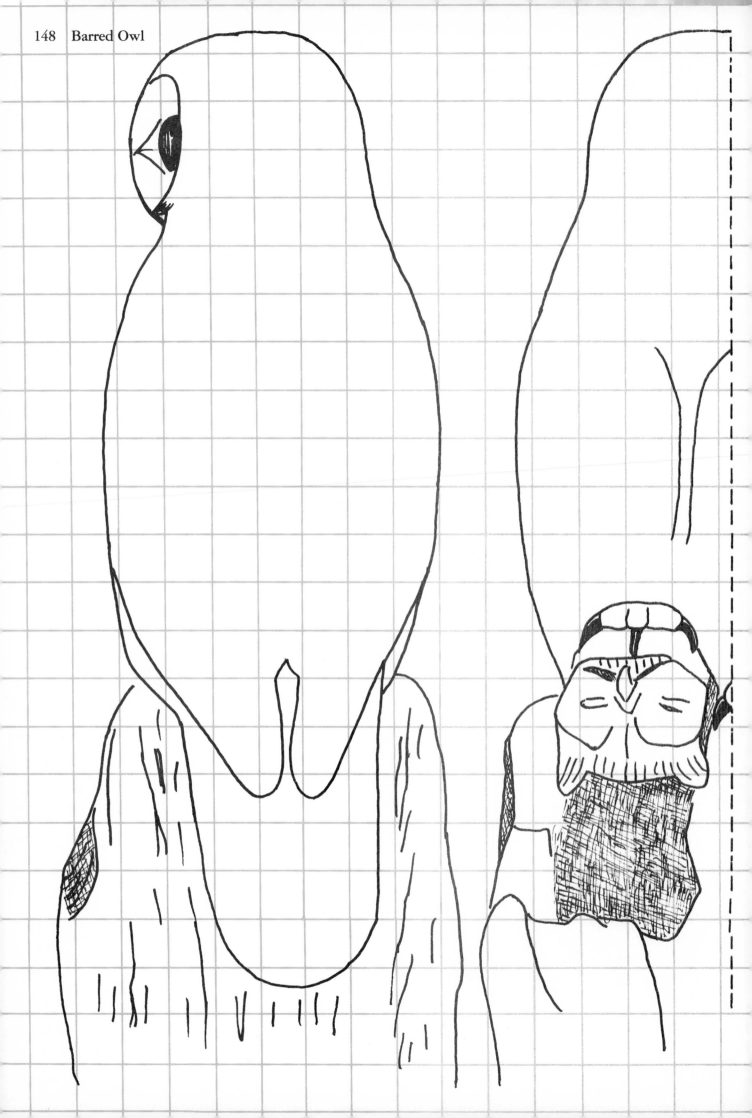

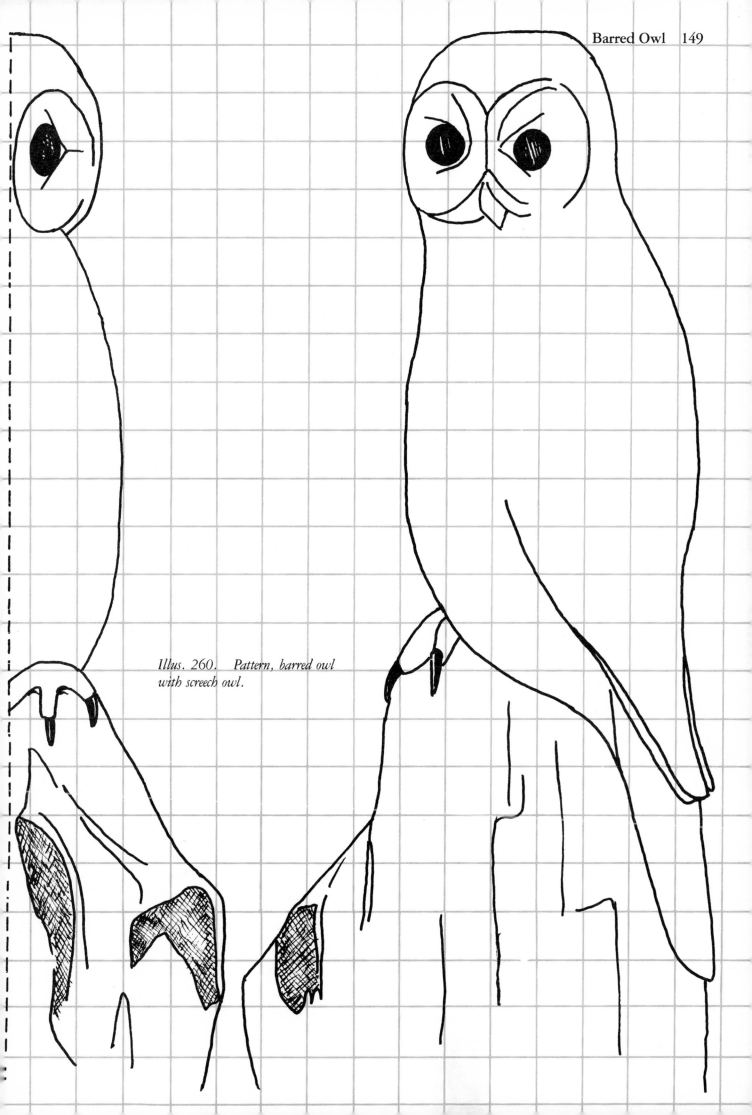

Illus. 260.   Pattern, barred owl with screech owl.

Parrot

The upper mandible of a parrot's beak is movable due to a hinge between the upper mandible and the skull. The lower mandible can slide. The beak muscles are very strong for cracking hard seeds and nuts. As pets, they can be trained to talk. Two toes point backward and two point forward.

Illus. 261.   Parrot in natural box elder.

Illus. 262.   Parrot, front view.

Illus. 263.   Parrot, side view.

Illus. 264.   Rear view.

Illus. 265–268.   Respective views showing initial rough cutting.

Illus. 266.   Front view.

Illus. 267.   Side view.

Illus. 268.   Rear view.

Illus. 269–272.   The second phase of rough carving in the same views, respectively, as Illus. 265–268.

Illus. 270.   Front view.

Illus. 271.   Side view.

Illus. 272.   Rear view.

Illus. 273.   Gouge-texturing the
surfaces of the base.

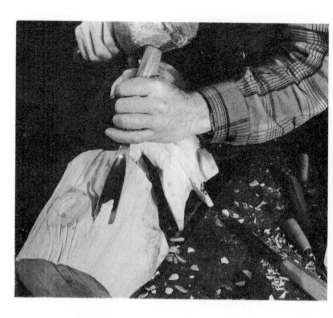

Illus. 274.   Carving a knot hole
into the base.

Illus. 275.   Completed base showing carved knots.

Illus. 276.   Close-up of parrot
head.

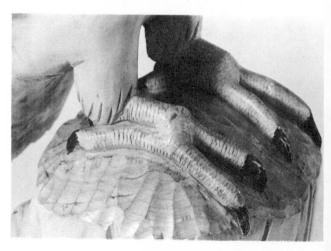

Illus. 277.   Close-up of feet and
claws. Note: Textured lines of feet
are done with a special tool.

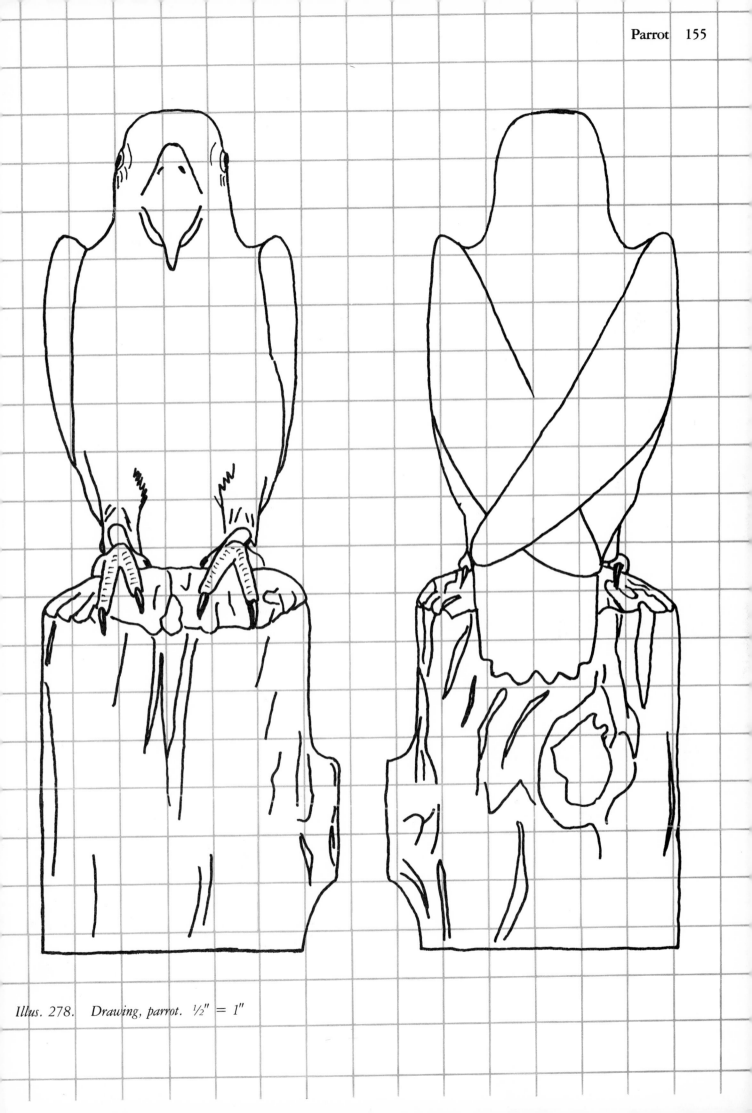

Illus. 278.   Drawing, parrot. ½" = 1"

Illus. 278.   Side view.

Scarlet Macaw

Macaws are the largest of the parrots. Almost all macaws live in forests. They have strong beaks that can crack open nuts and seeds. The beak is also used for grasping and climbing. They are very beautiful birds.

Illus. 279–282. Scarlet macaw of natural box elder. Initial roughing cuts.

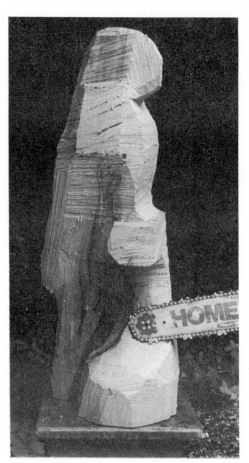

Illus. 280. Side view.

Illus. 281. Side view.

Illus. 282. Rear view.

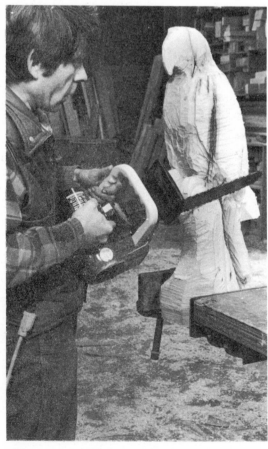

Illus. 283. Further roughing out with the electric chain saw.

Illus. 284. Final chain-sawn front view.

Illus. 285.   Final chain-sawn side view.

Illus. 286.   Shaping feathers with electric die grinder.

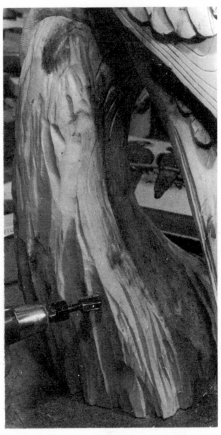

Illus. 287.   Contouring base with the die grinder.

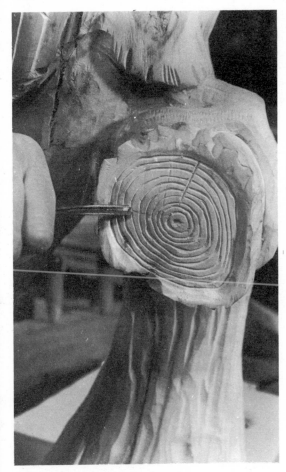

Illus. 288.   Carving end-grain and fake crack with the v-parting tool.

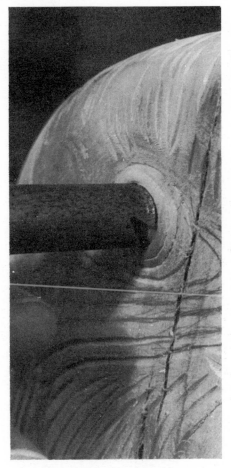

Illus. 289.   Forming eye with special tool. See pages 24–25.

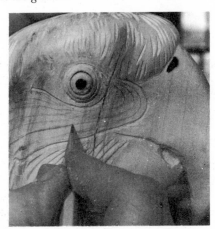

Illus. 290.   Pencil in the side of the head details.

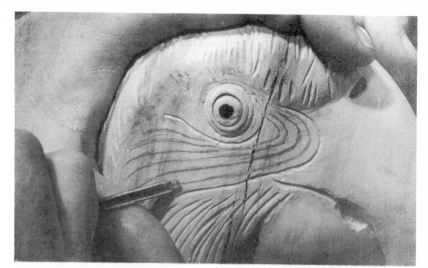

*Illus. 291.   Accent lines with
v-parting tool as shown.*

*Illus. 292–293.   Carving the
shoulder area feathers with the
v-parting tool.*

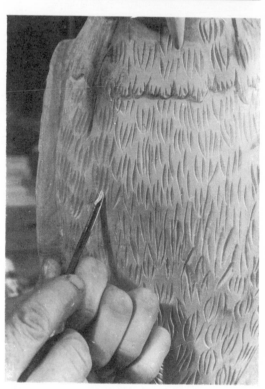

*Illus. 294.   Simulating breast
feathers with small v-parting tool.*

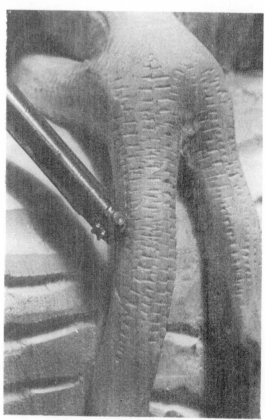

*Illus. 295.   Texturing foot surfaces
with special homemade tool. Refer to
page 30.*

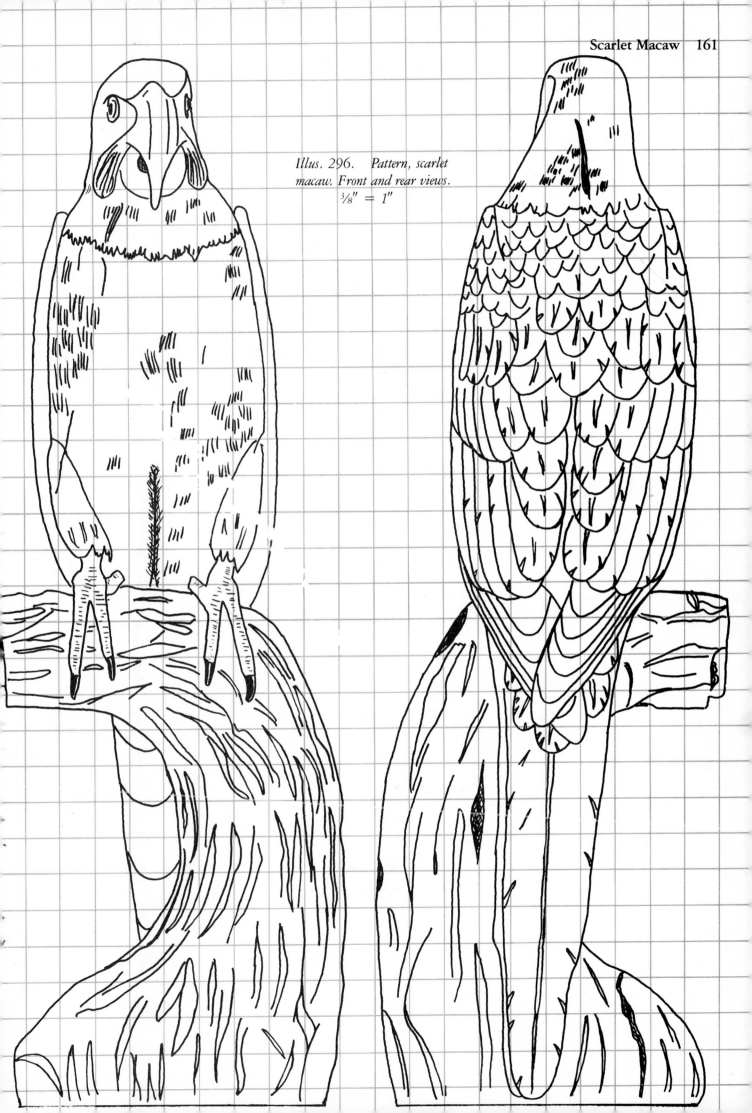

Illus. 296. Pattern, scarlet macaw. Front and rear views.
⅜" = 1"

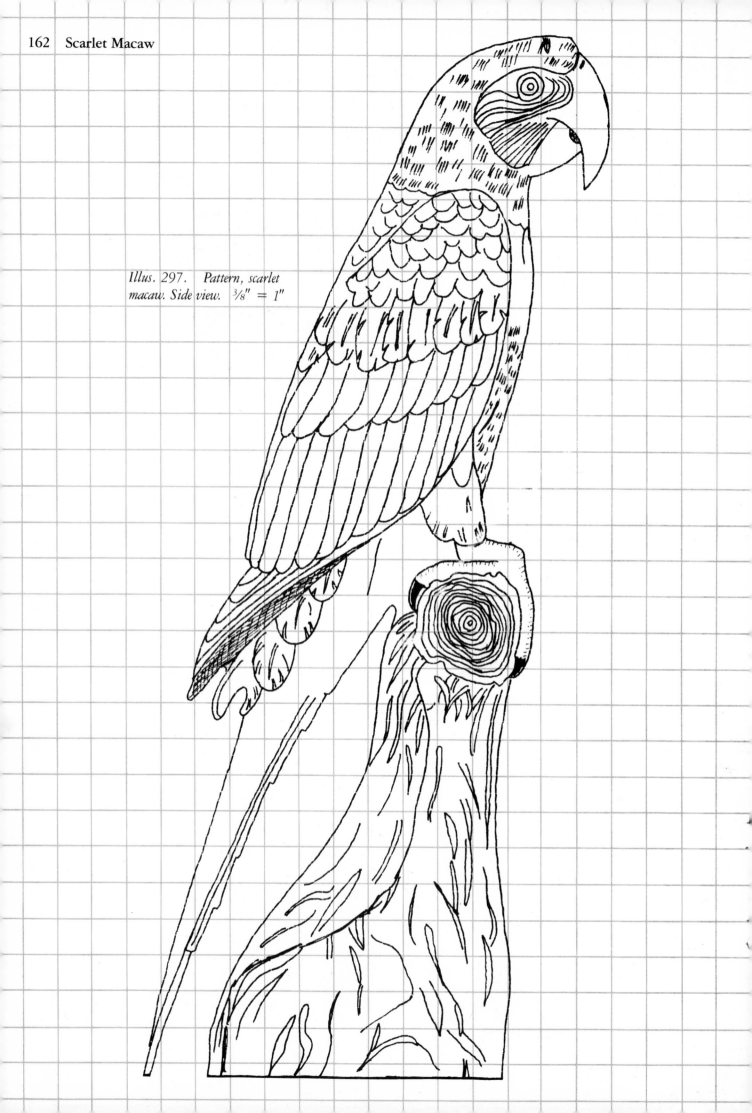

Illus. 297. Pattern, scarlet macaw. Side view. ³⁄₈″ = 1″

Bald Eagle

Bald eagles are majestic and very symbolic birds. They build their nests in large trees and sometimes in or on cliffs, with sticks, roots, plant stalks, twigs, etc. Their food consists largely of fish along with some birds, mammals, and carrion.

Illus. 298.   Bald eagle with a brown trout in stained box elder.

Illus. 299.   Bald eagle. Front view.

Illus. 300–301.   Bald eagle. Side views.

Illus. 302.   Rear view.

Illus. 303–305.   Various views of chain-sawn rough carvings.

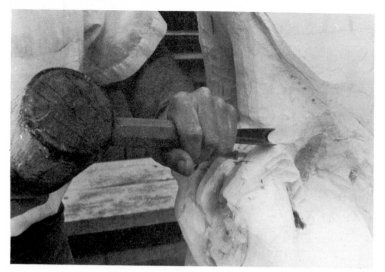

Illus. 306.   Carving the leg-to-talon area with a gouge.

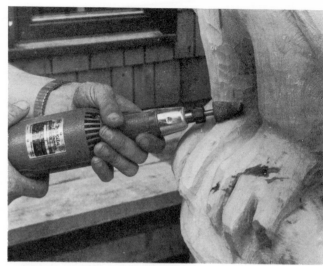

Illus. 307.   Instead of a gouge, use a die grinder and carbide cutter, as shown.

Illus. 308.   Smoothing rough cuts with a disk sander.

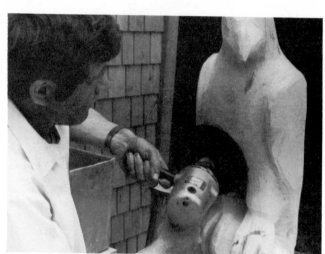

Illus. 309–310.   Carving ready for final detailing.

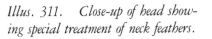

Illus. 311.   Close-up of head showing special treatment of neck feathers.

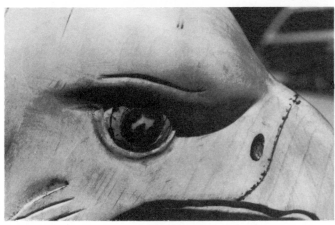

Illus. 312.   Close-up of eye carving
and shading with the wood-burning
tool.

Illus. 313.   "Dots" on brown trout
are wood-burned.

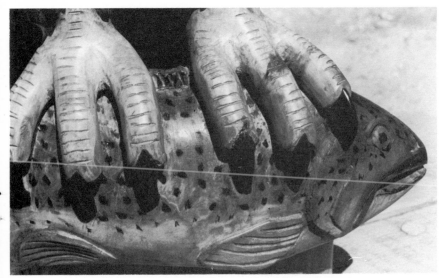

Illus. 314.   Another view of the
brown trout carving.

Illus. 315.   View of tail and wing
feather shapes.

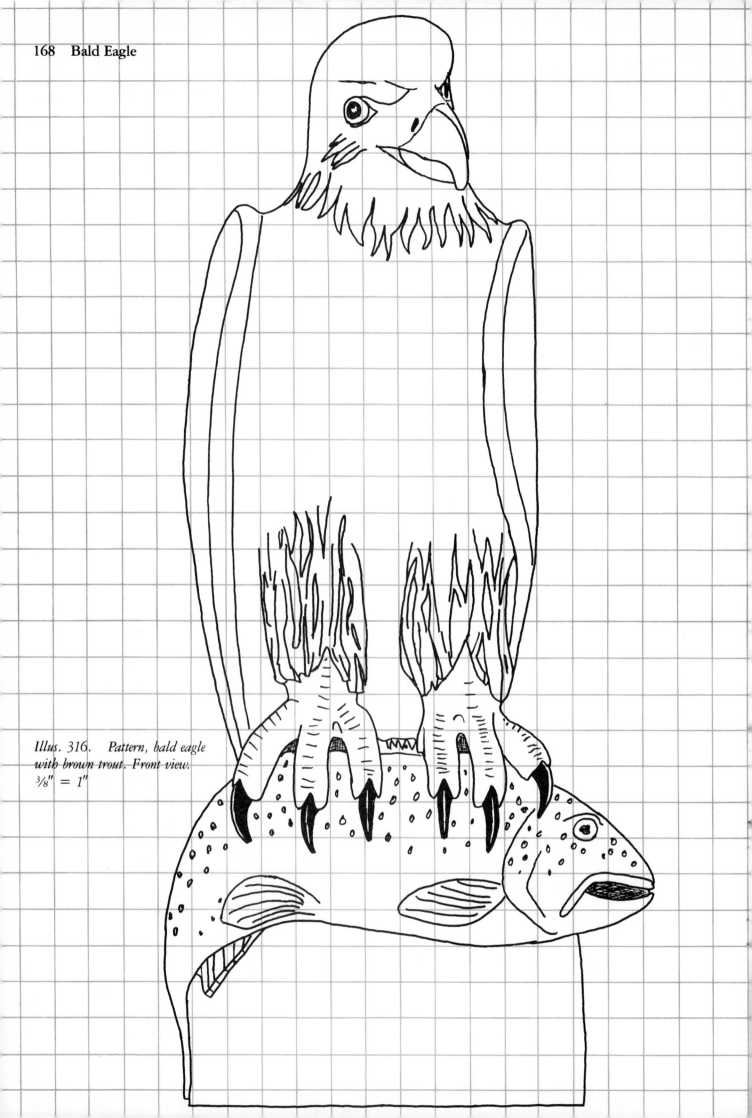

Illus. 316.   Pattern, bald eagle with brown trout. Front view.
³⁄₈" = 1"

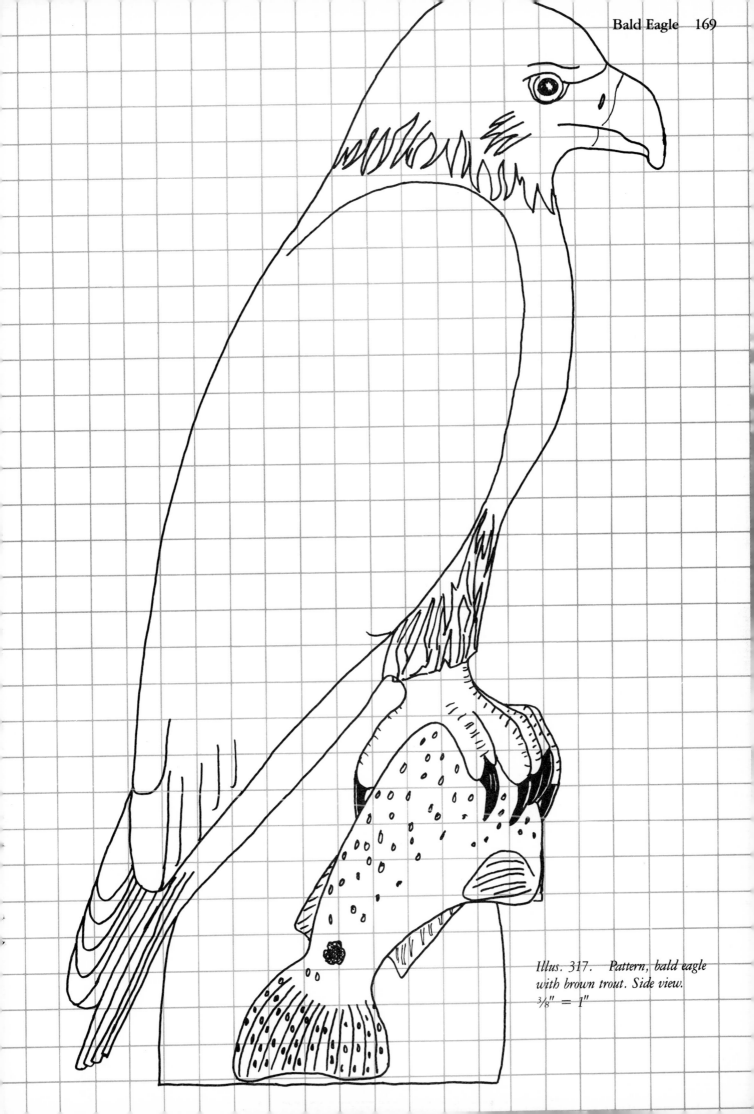

*Illus. 317.   Pattern, bald eagle
with brown trout. Side view.*
$3/8'' = 1''$

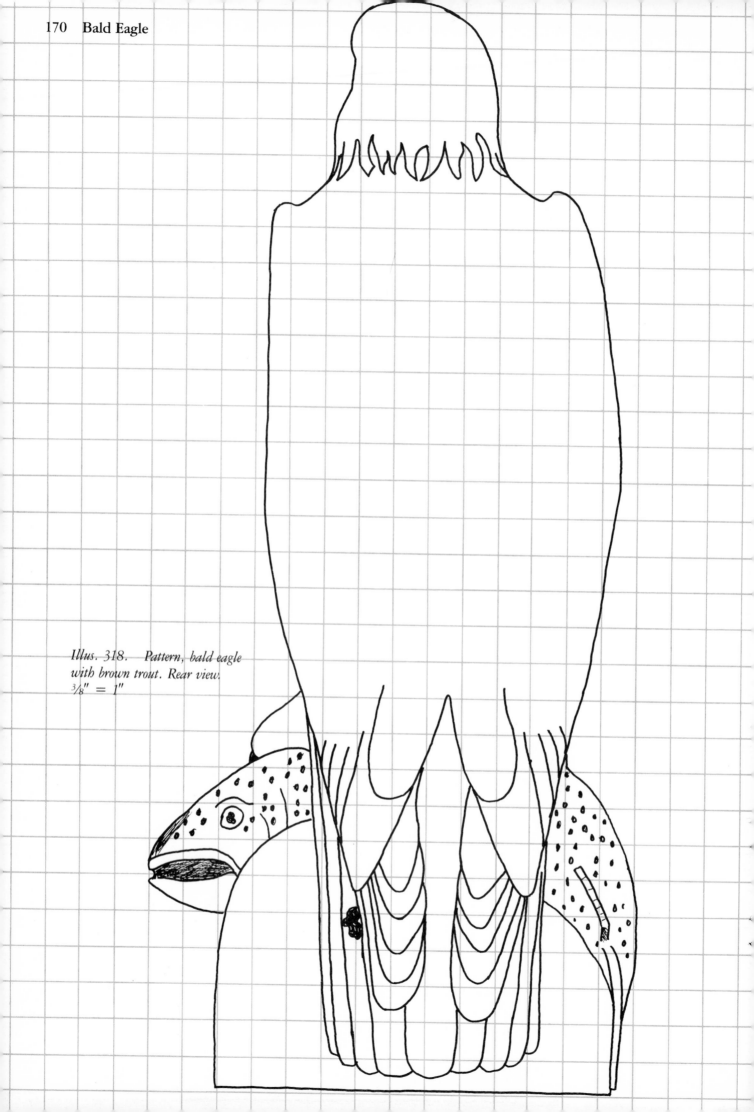

Illus. 318. Pattern, bald eagle with brown trout. Rear view.
$3/8'' = 1''$

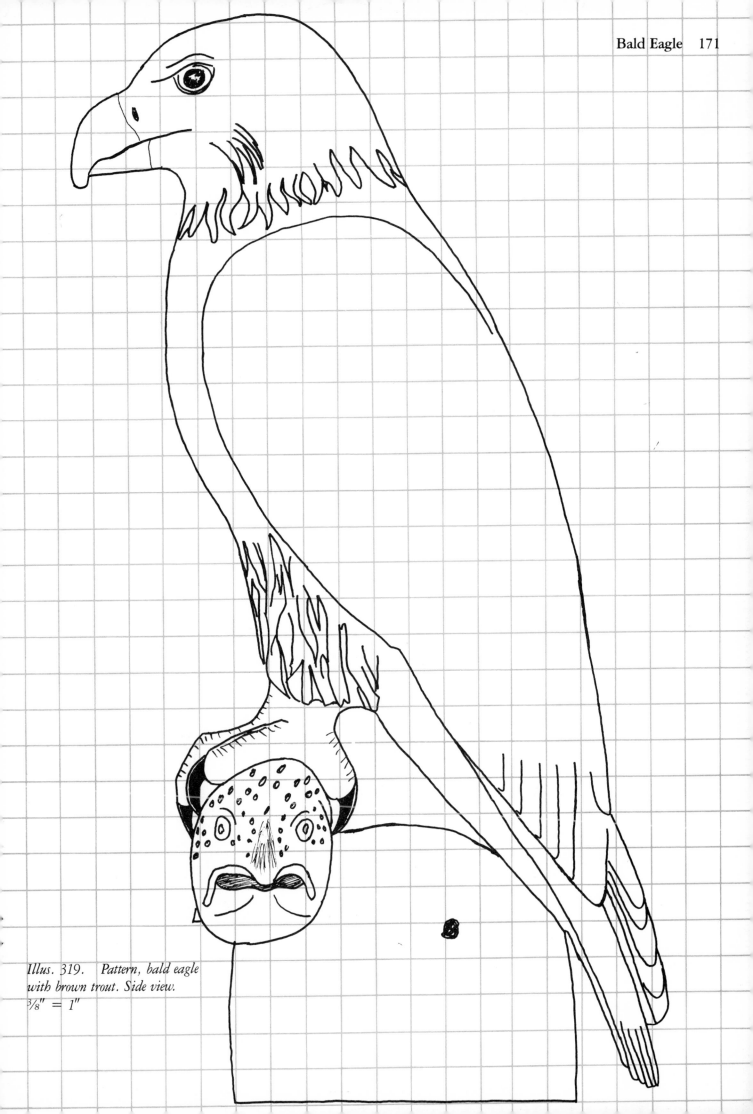

Illus. 319.   Pattern, bald eagle with brown trout. Side view.
$^3/_8" = 1"$

Illus. 320. Bald eagle including the base is carved from one piece of white ash.

Illus. 321. Front view of bald eagle.

Illus. 322–323. Side views.

Illus. 324. Rear view.

Illus. 325–326.   Roughing out with the chain saw.

Illus. 327.   Close-up showing light cuts made with the chain saw maneuvered in a "rasping action" to shape the neck close to final size.

Illus. 328.   Inside of wings are also "rasped" with the chain saw in the final roughing-out stages.

Illus. 329.   Front view of roughed-out bird.

Illus. 330.   Rear view. Notice the nonsymmetrical shape.

Illus. 331–332.   Side views of the roughed-out eagle.

Illus. 333.   Shaping the inside wing feathers with the die grinder.

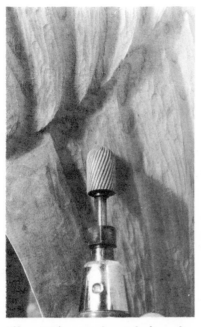

Illus. 334. *A closeup look at the feather-shaping with the steel-cutting burr and the texture it produces.*

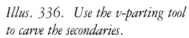
Illus. 335. *Marking the secondary feathers.*

Illus. 336. *Use the v-parting tool to carve the secondaries.*

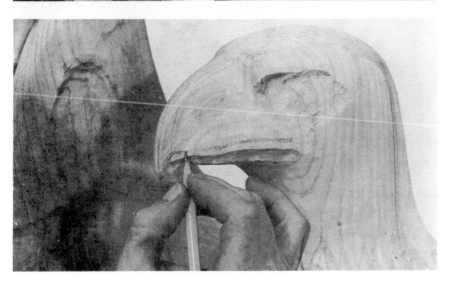

Illus. 337. *Carving the "feather breaks" of tail.*

Illus. 338. *Laying out the mandible separation.*

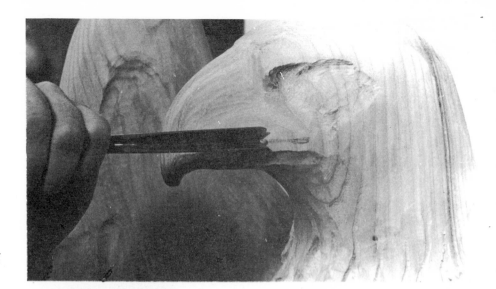

Illus. 339.   Using the v-parting tool to give definition to the beak.

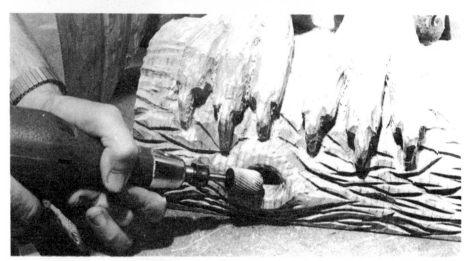

Illus. 340.   Forming a knot on the base.

Illus. 341.   Hollowing the end of a carved branch on the base.

Illus. 342.   Wood-burning tool is used on beak, its nostril, and on the eye to bring the carving alive.

Illus. 343.   The wood-burning tool makes realistic annular rings in this carved log base. Notice texturing to represent bark.

Illus. 344.   A good look at the finished base. Notice simulated checks that can be carved or wood-burned.

Illus. 345.   Apply thinned, white oil paint to the head.

Illus. 347.   Body is stained with a medium-walnut danish oil.

Illus. 346.   View of finished head.

Illus. 348.   View of completed rear-feather detailing. Tail feathers are finished like the head with thinned white oil base paint.

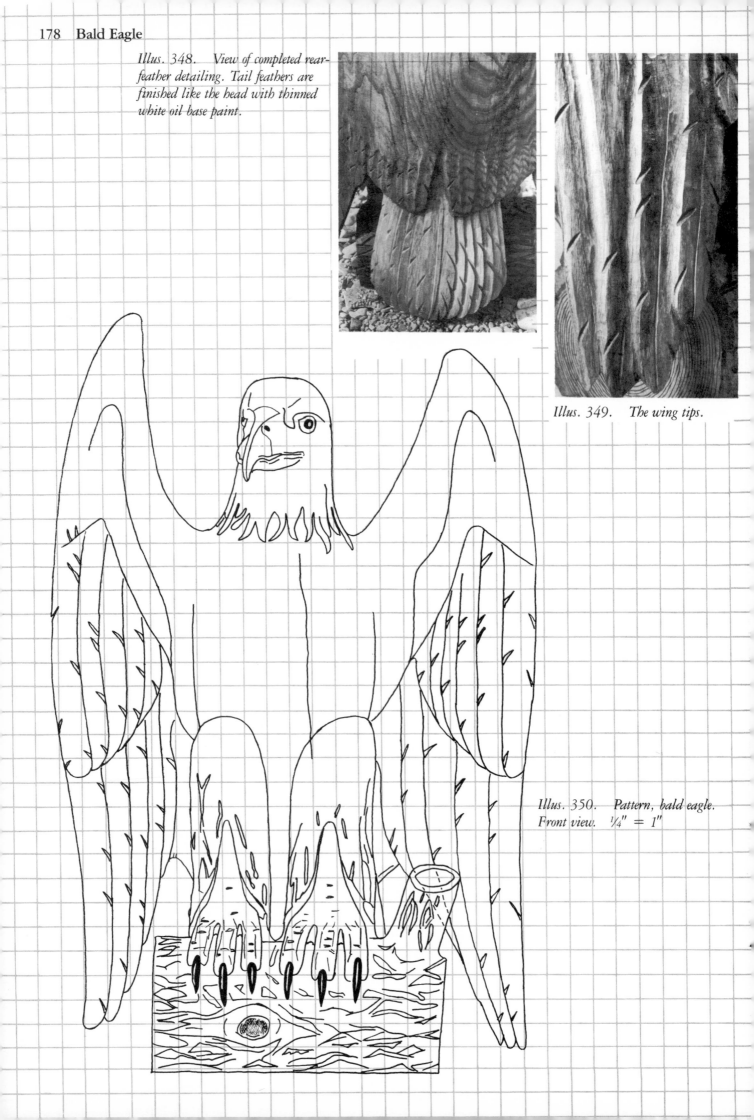

Illus. 349.   The wing tips.

Illus. 350.   Pattern, bald eagle. Front view.   ¼" = 1"

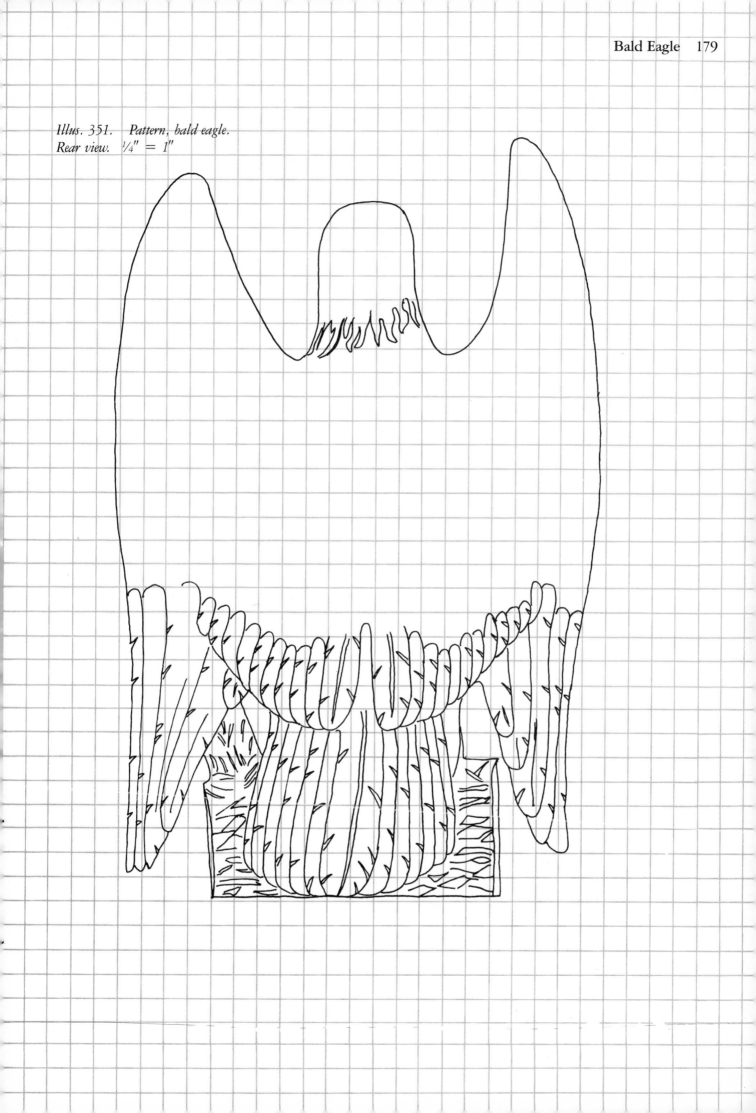

Illus. 351.   Pattern, bald eagle. Rear view.   ¼" = 1"

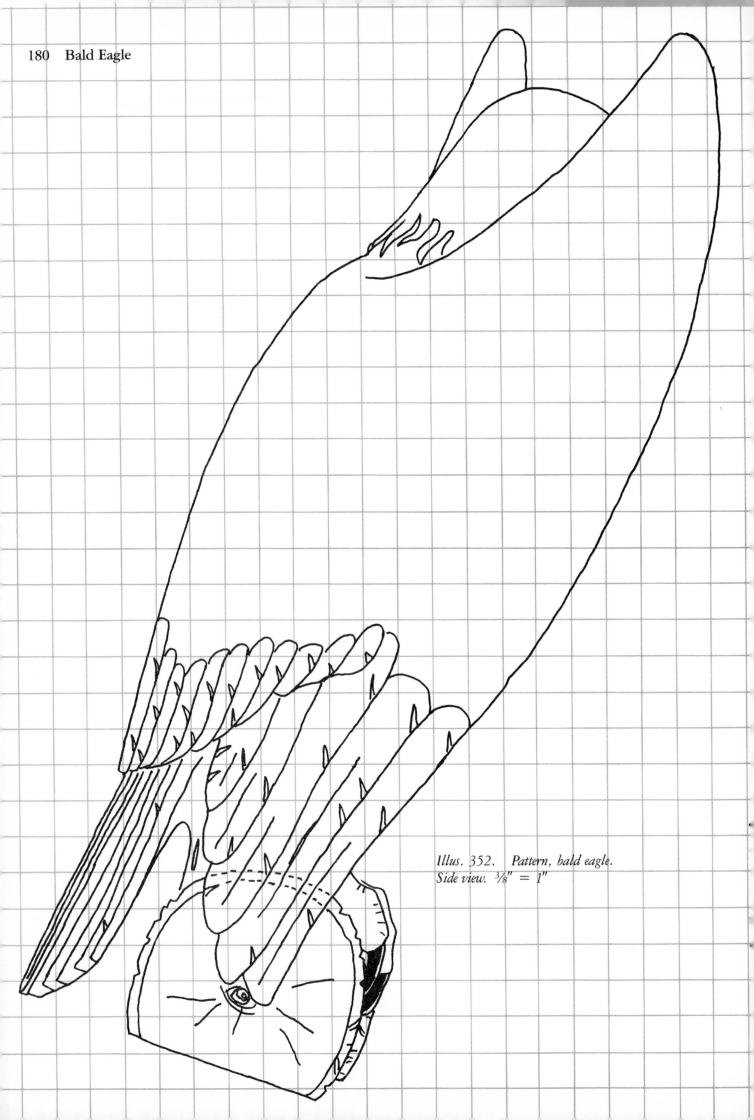

Illus. 352.   Pattern, bald eagle.
Side view. $\frac{3}{8}'' = 1''$

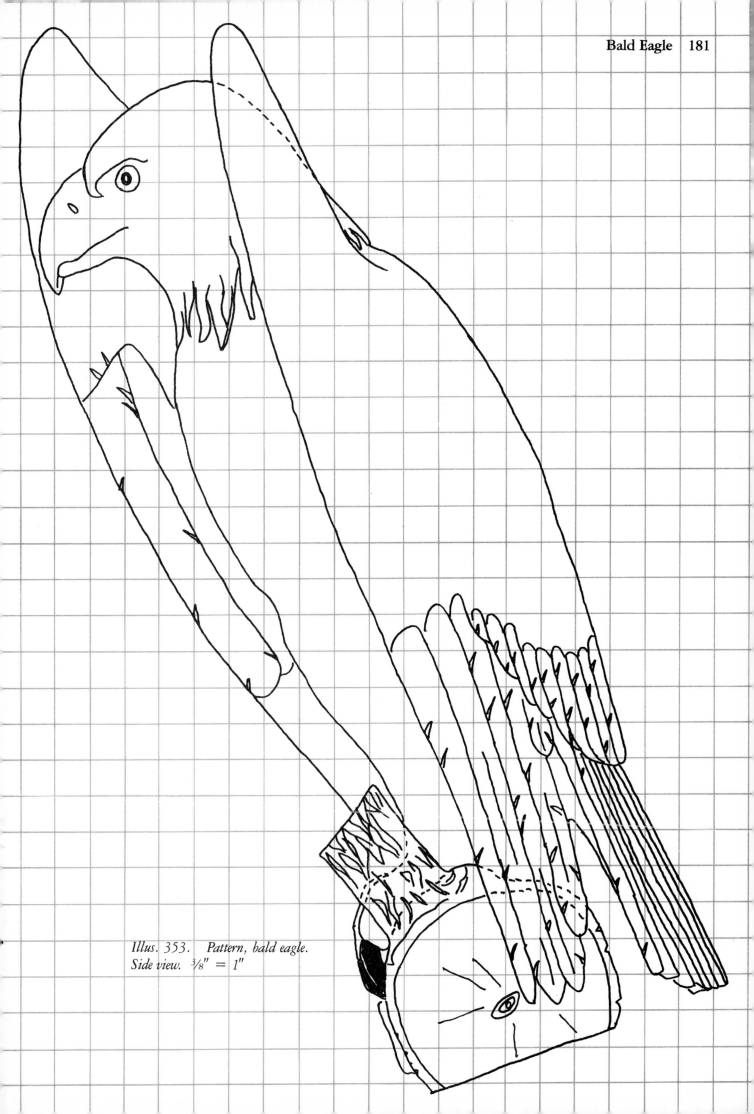

Illus. 353.   Pattern, bald eagle.
Side view. ³/₈" = 1"

Golden Eagle

The nest sites of golden eagles include crags, cliffs, and trees. The nest is usually constructed of sticks, twigs, grass, and the like. They prey upon fairly good-sized birds and animals such as prairie dogs, ground squirrels, rabbits, waterfowl, and grouse.

Illus. 355.   Eyes are walnut dowels set into a through hole.

Illus. 354.   Golden eagle of stained white cedar measures 30" long by 41" high with the base.

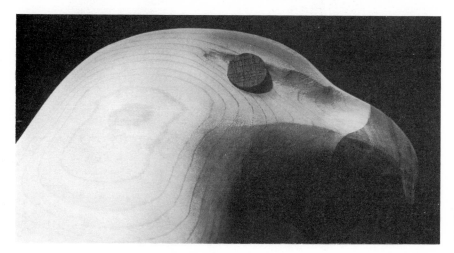

Illus. 356.   The bill is also walnut. It was custom-fitted to the contoured joint with bandsaw and file-fitted, then glued in place with epoxy.

Illus. 357.   Base with legs and feet carved from the same piece.

Illus. 358.   Matching openings in body were cut with a portable router.

Illus. 359 (above).   View showing the back of the head and neck area.

Illus. 360 (right).   Tail and wing-tip shapes.

Illus. 361 (far right).   Starting the final shaping of the bill.

Illus. 362.   Side view showing profile shaping nearly completed.

Illus. 363–364.   Views of the head details.

Illus. 365.   A look at the contours from a different angle.

Illus. 366.   Finished tail area. The tail feathers were "colored" by wood-burning their surfaces with a burning tool.

Illus. 367–368.   Base and feet area surfaces of the claws were also wood-burned.

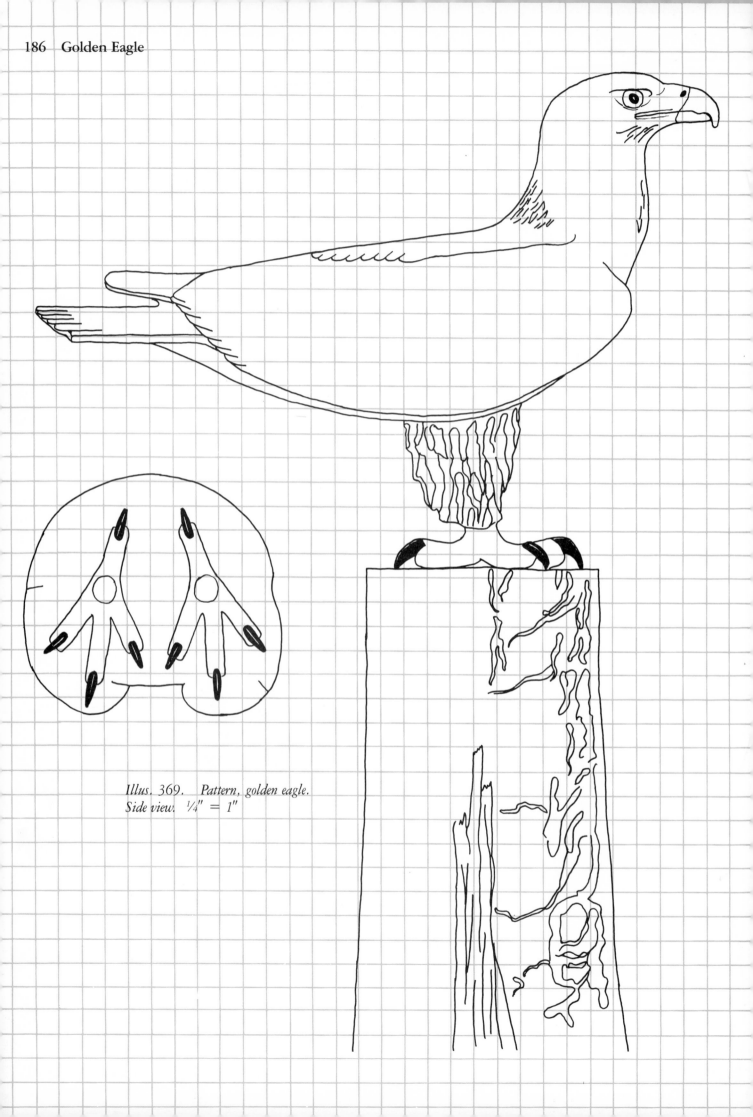

Illus. 369.   Pattern, golden eagle.
Side view. ¼" = 1"

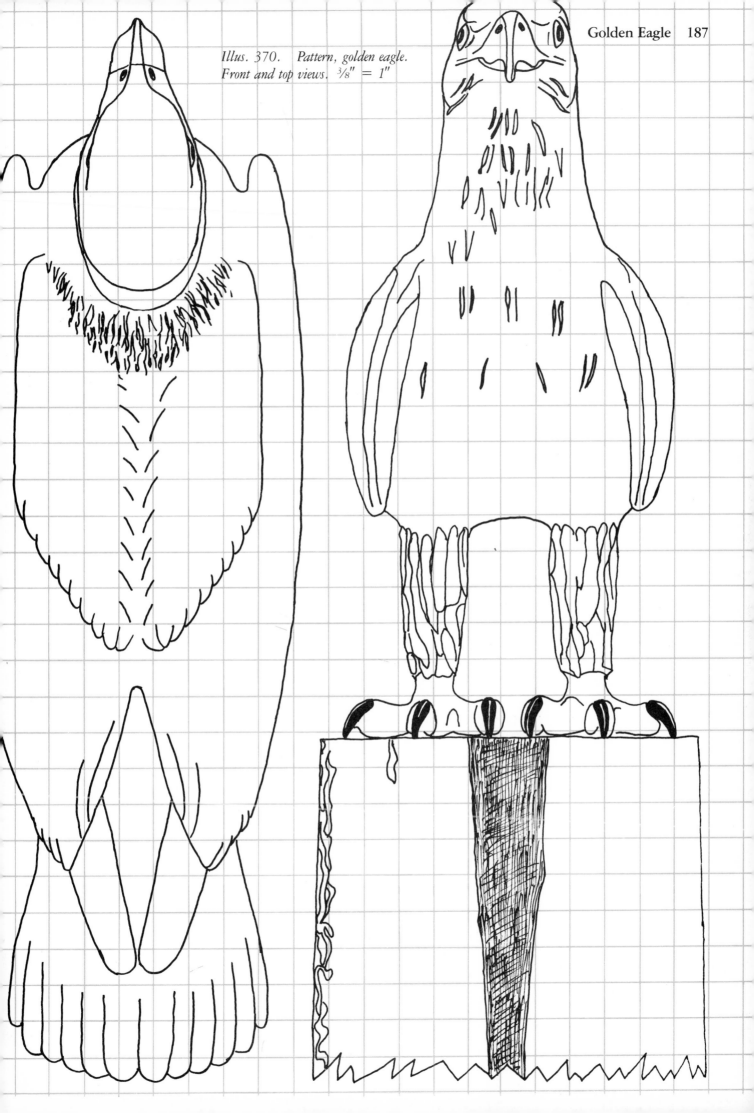

Illus. 370.   Pattern, golden eagle.
Front and top views. ³⁄₈″ = 1″

Great Blue Heron

The great blue heron is a large stately bird, with long legs. Its prey includes fish, frogs, small snakes, salamanders, mice, and other small mammals as well as grasshoppers and water insects. It will stand motionless, in water, neck drawn back in an "s" shape, waiting until a fish or something else gets in range. Then it will strike with a lightning-fast stroke of the sharp beak. It will also stalk its prey. Nests are usually in tall trees and made of sticks, twigs, and dry grass.

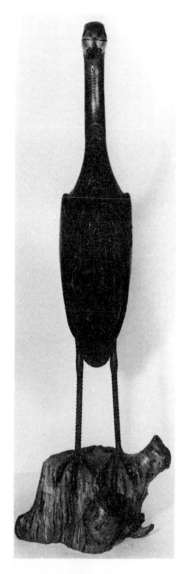

Illus. 371.   Front view of the blue heron in butternut on steel legs. It stands 43" high.

Illus. 372–373.   Side views of the blue heron.

Illus. 375.   Head roughed out— note the joint giving a change in grain direction. It is dowelled and glued.

Illus. 374.   Rear view.

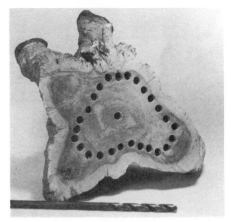

Illus. 376.   Working on the breast feathers. Note *holes bored for legs of metal rods.*

Illus. 377.   The carved breast feathers.

Illus. 378.   Holes are drilled in the bottom of this ironwood base to minimize cracking or check stresses.

Illus. 379.   Concrete reinforcement rod ("re-bar") in the two sizes used to make the legs and feet.

Illus. 380.   Here's the bent and arc-welded assembly for legs and feet.

Illus. 381.   View showing the rugged base and the metal work.

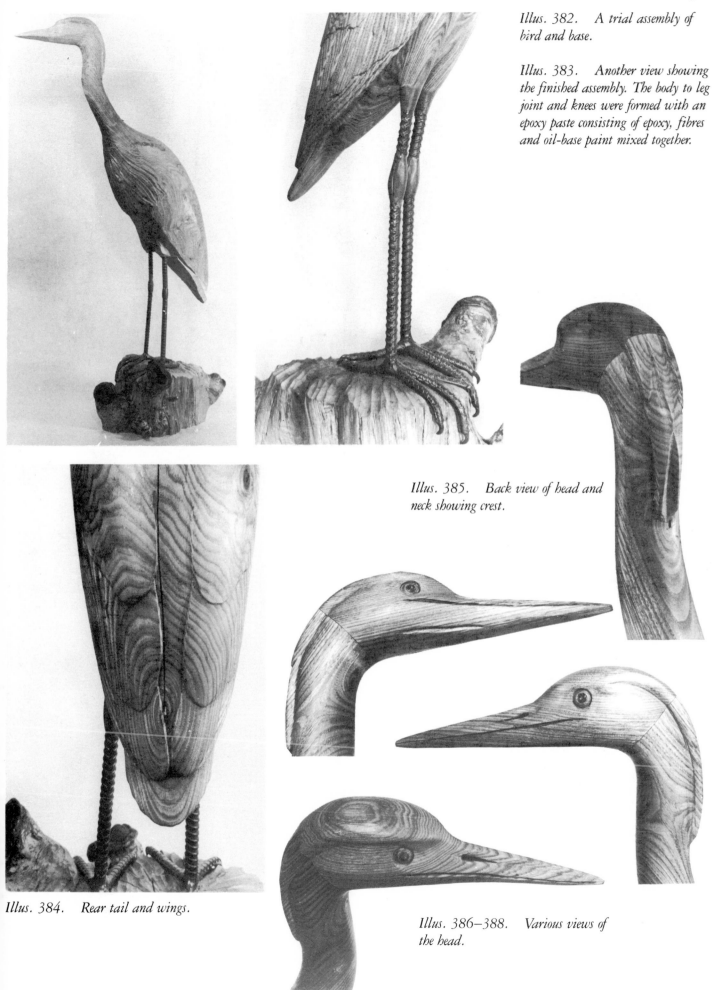

Illus. 382.   A trial assembly of bird and base.

Illus. 383.   Another view showing the finished assembly. The body to leg joint and knees were formed with an epoxy paste consisting of epoxy, fibres and oil-base paint mixed together.

Illus. 385.   Back view of head and neck showing crest.

Illus. 384.   Rear tail and wings.

Illus. 386–388.   Various views of the head.

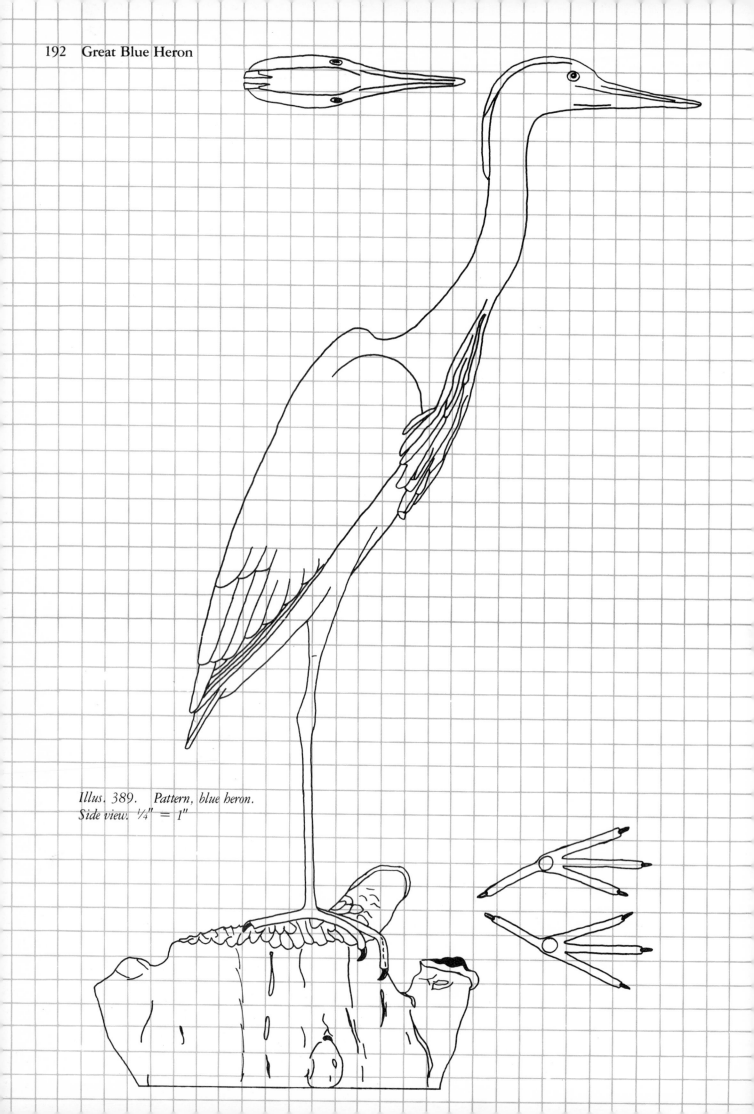

Illus. 389.   Pattern, blue heron.
Side view. ¼" = 1"

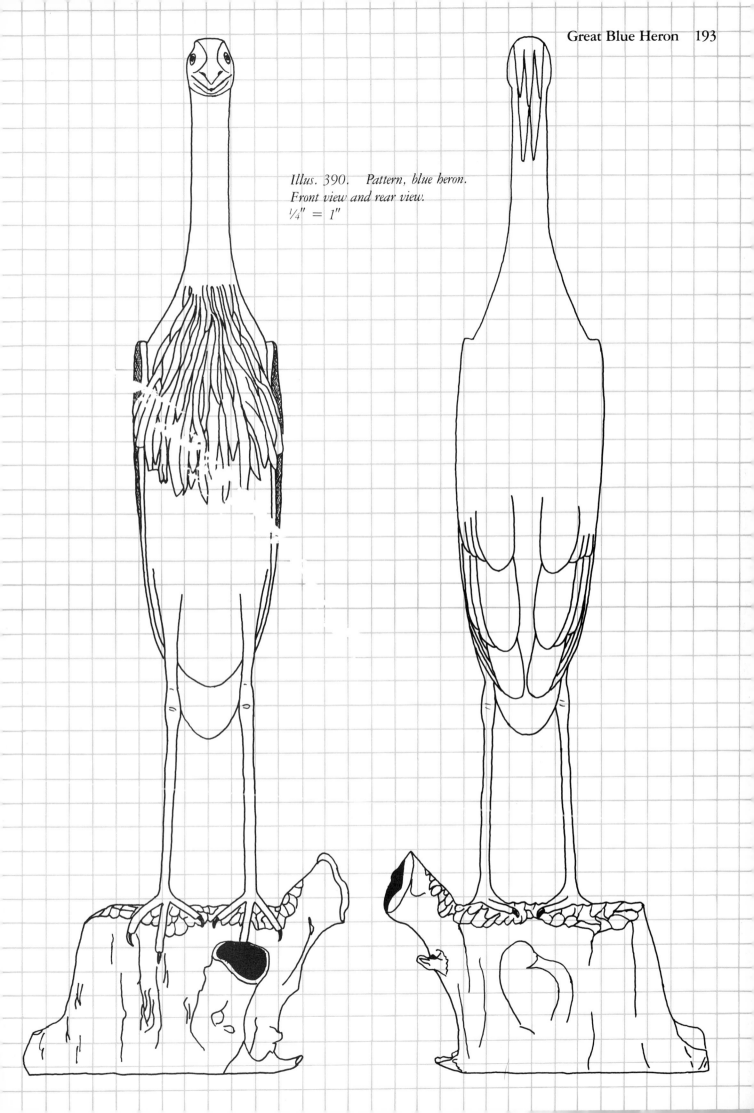

Illus. 390. Pattern, blue heron.
Front view and rear view.
¼″ = 1″

Illus. 391.   Blue heron, all carved from butternut log with added beak of zebra wood.

Illus. 392–393.   Side views.

Illus. 394.   Blue heron. Front view.

Illus. 395.   With log selected and cut to length, mark off body length.

Illus. 397.   Remove extra stock from the sides with vertical chain-saw cuts.

Illus. 398.   The head and shoulders are blocked-out next.

Illus. 396.   Use felt marker to outline the back view.

Illus. 399–400.   The front is notched as on the side-view drawing.

Illus. 401.   Front view of roughed-out work.

Illus. 402.   Side view as rough cut.

Illus. 403.   Back view, roughed-out.

Illus. 404.   Starting to rough-out feet.

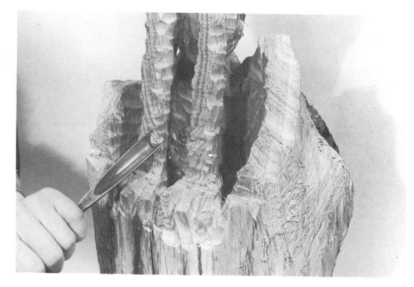

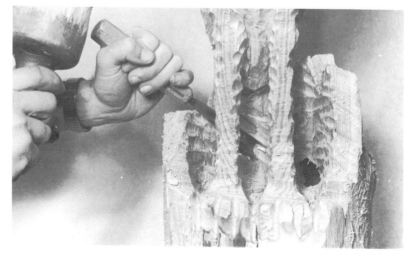

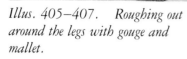

Illus. 405–407.   Roughing out around the legs with gouge and mallet.

Illus. 408.   Starting to thin the legs with the gouge.

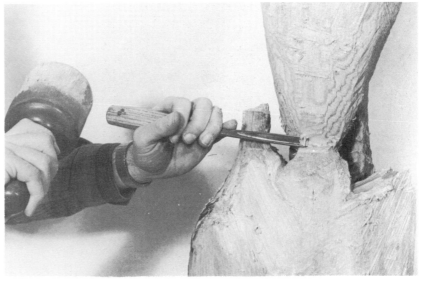

Illus. 409.   Tail is left connected to base for strength.

Illus. 410.   Here is a look at the progress so far.

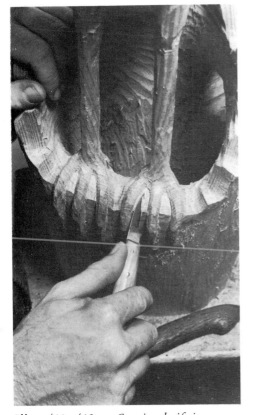

Illus. 411–412.   Carving knife is used to accentuate toes and legs. Note hollowed-out base, which was essentially cut away with the chain saw.

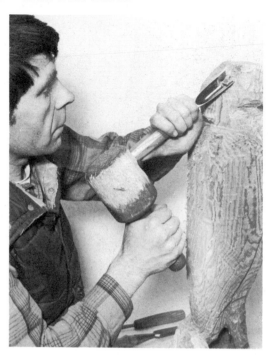

Illus. 413.   Starting to shape the head.

Illus. 414.   Deepening the "s" curve of the neck with the v-parting tool.

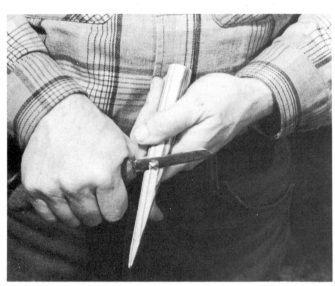

Illus. 415.   Giving the beak its preliminary shape.

Illus. 416.   Here is how the beak is set and glued into a hole in the head.

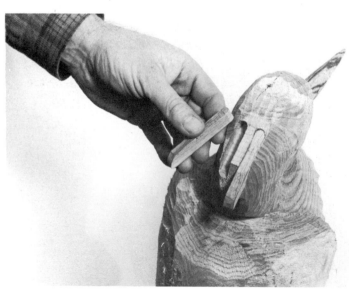

Illus. 417.   Two pieces are set into router-cut grooves for the crest.

Illus. 418.   Shaping the head and beak intersection with a carving knife.

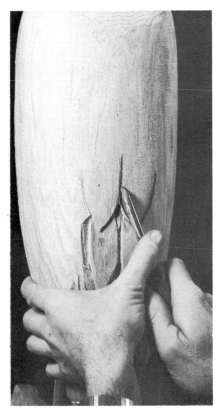

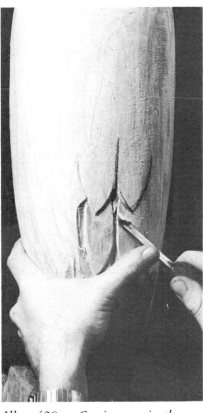

Illus. 419.   Following pencil lines with a knife to carve a feather.

Illus. 420.   Cutting to raise the feathers in relief.

Illus. 421.   Once carved, sand the feathers individually.

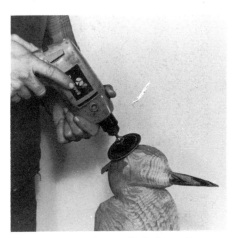

Illus. 424.   The small disk sander is used for final shaping as well as initial sanding.

Illus. 423.   The v-parting tool also works for carving the plumes.

Illus. 422.   Carving the plumes of the neck and lower breast.

Illus. 425.   Small v-parting tool cuts the separation of the bill.

Illus. 426.   Cleaning up the cross-grained fibres of the butternut with a sharp knife.

Illus. 427.   Making another line required for the heron beak.

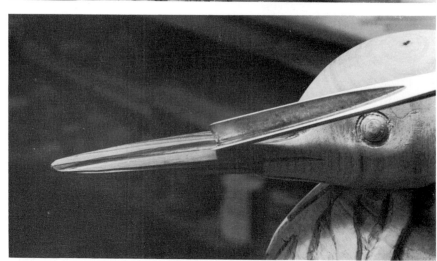

Illus. 428.   Woodburning to darken the pupil.

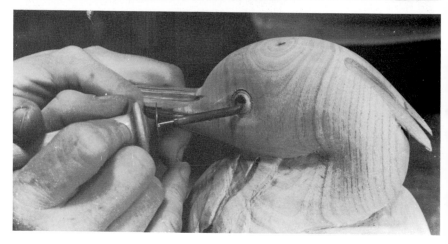

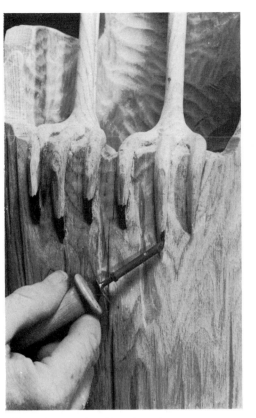

Illus. 429. *Woodburning the claws.*

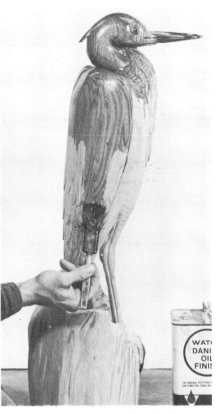

Illus. 430. *Natural danish oil makes the perfect finish for butternut.*

Illus. 431. *The finished legs and feet.*

Illus. 433. *Finished tail.*

Illus. 432. *The finished breast area.*

Illus. 434.   View of the completed head.

Illus. 435.   View showing the finished crest inserts.

Illus. 436.   Close-up, showing use of three different size eye tools to create this particular eye.

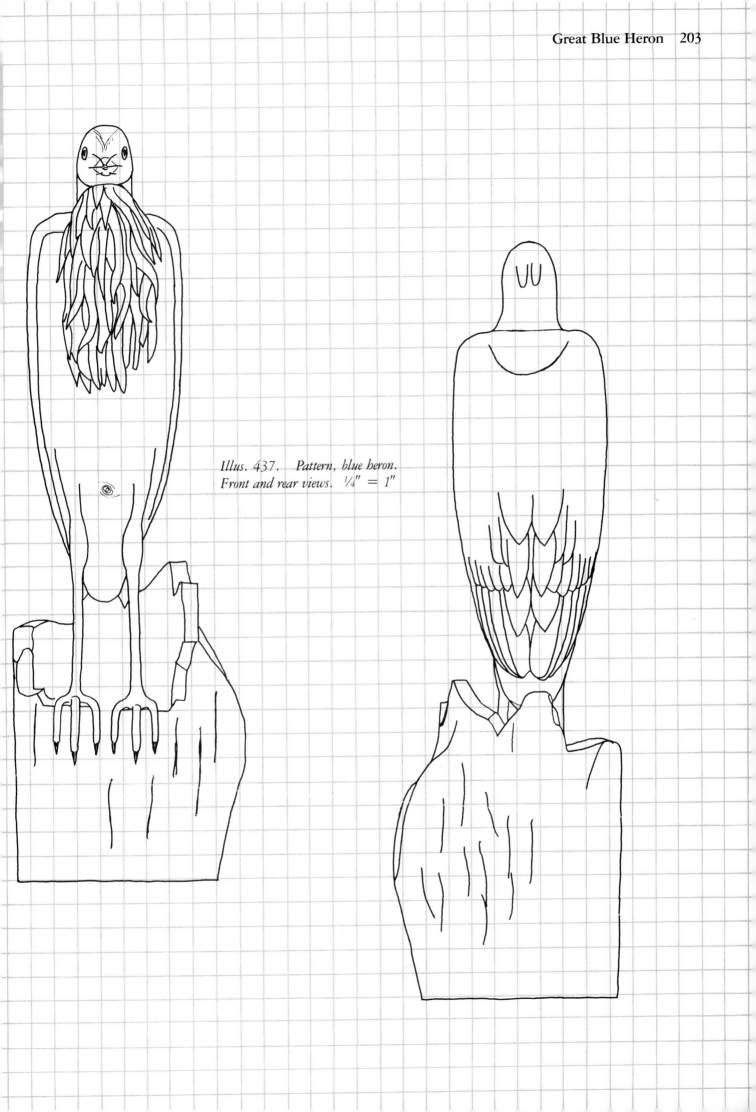

*Illus. 437. Pattern, blue heron.
Front and rear views. ¼" = 1"*

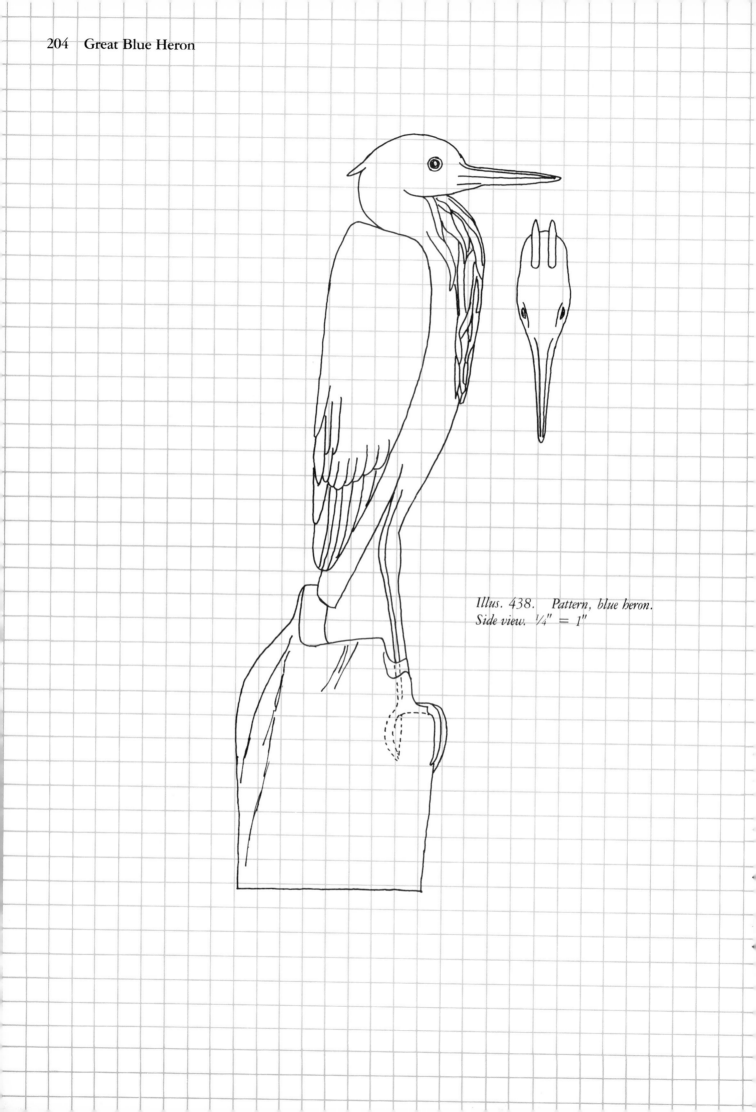

Illus. 438.   Pattern, blue heron.
Side view. ¼" = 1"

Flamingo (Scarlet or American)

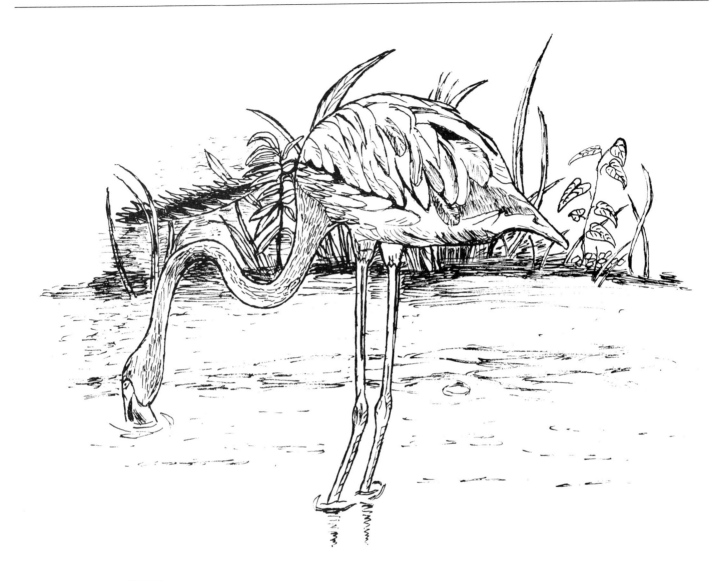

Flamingoes have long necks and very long legs. The "knee" of a bird is actually the "ankle." Males and females look similar. Their nests are made of heaped-up mud along with stones, shells, grass, feathers, and the like. All flamingoes sift food from water with a specialized beak. It is a filtration apparatus with areas inside the beak having lammellae which filter out small crustacea, algae and unicellular organisms. Because of this system, hardly any other birds compete with flamingoes for food.

Illus. 439.   Flamingo of laminated cedar stands an impressive 4' tall.

Illus. 440.   Front view, flamingo.

Illus. 441.   Rear view.

Illus. 442–443.   Side views.

Illus. 444.   Laminated blocks ready for cutting.

Illus. 445.   Cutting the head and neck from one block.

Illus. 446.   Cutting the side profile shape of the body.

Illus. 447.   With scrap pieces taped back together, the top-view shape of the body is sawn on the bandsaw to complete the compound-cutting.

Illus. 448.   This shows the result of compound-sawing the body shape.

Illus. 449.   Typical dowel and glue joint connects the neck to the body.

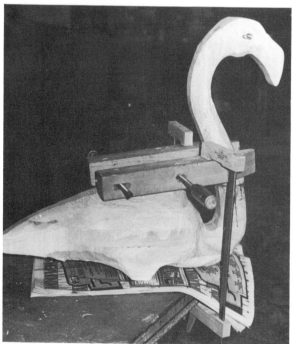

Illus. 450.   One way to clamp the assembly for a tight joint is shown here on a corner of the workbench.

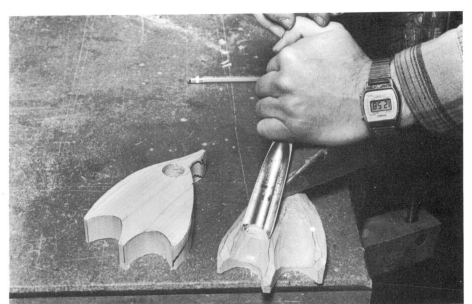

Illus. 451.   Gouge-shaping the web feet.

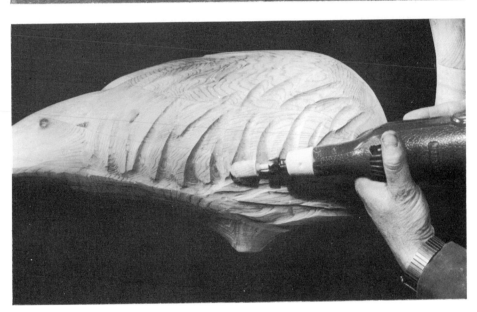

Illus. 452.   Working the body, drooping side feathers with the die grinder.

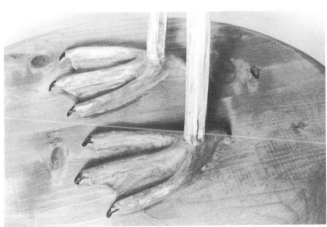

Illus. 453.   Here, legs carved from maple saplings (selected for natural bends at knees) are inserted through holes in web feet, which extend into the base.

Illus. 454.   Flamingo head. Note that beak tip is stained.

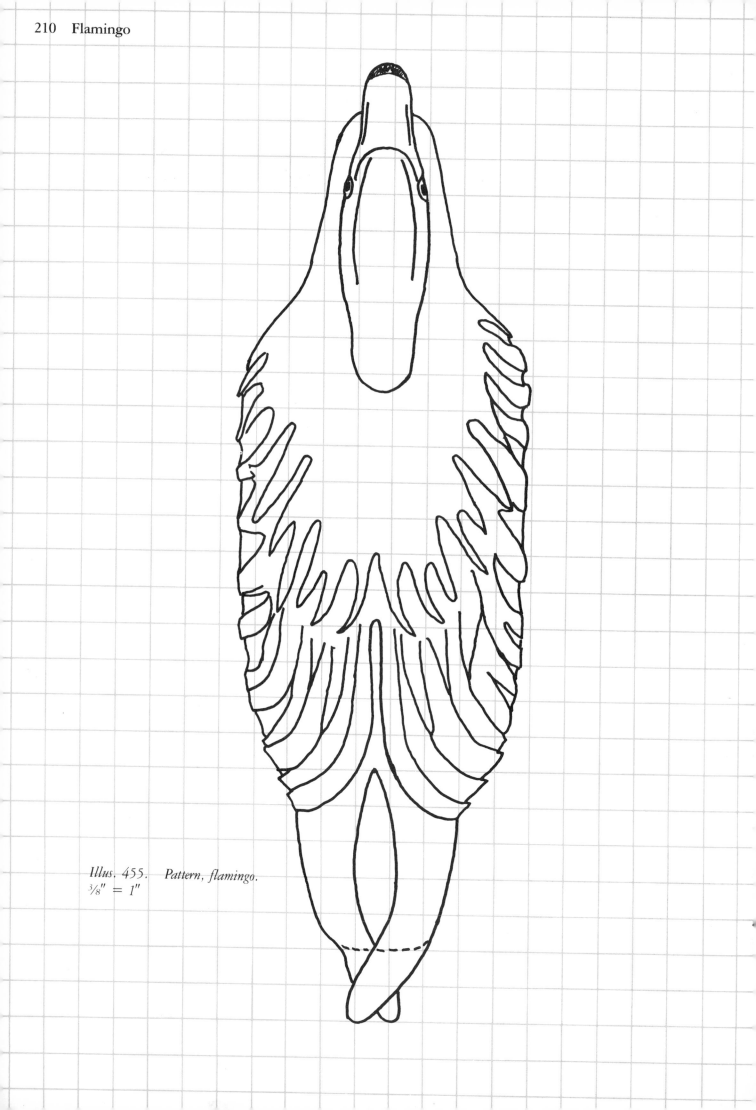

Illus. 455.　Pattern, flamingo.
3/8″ = 1″

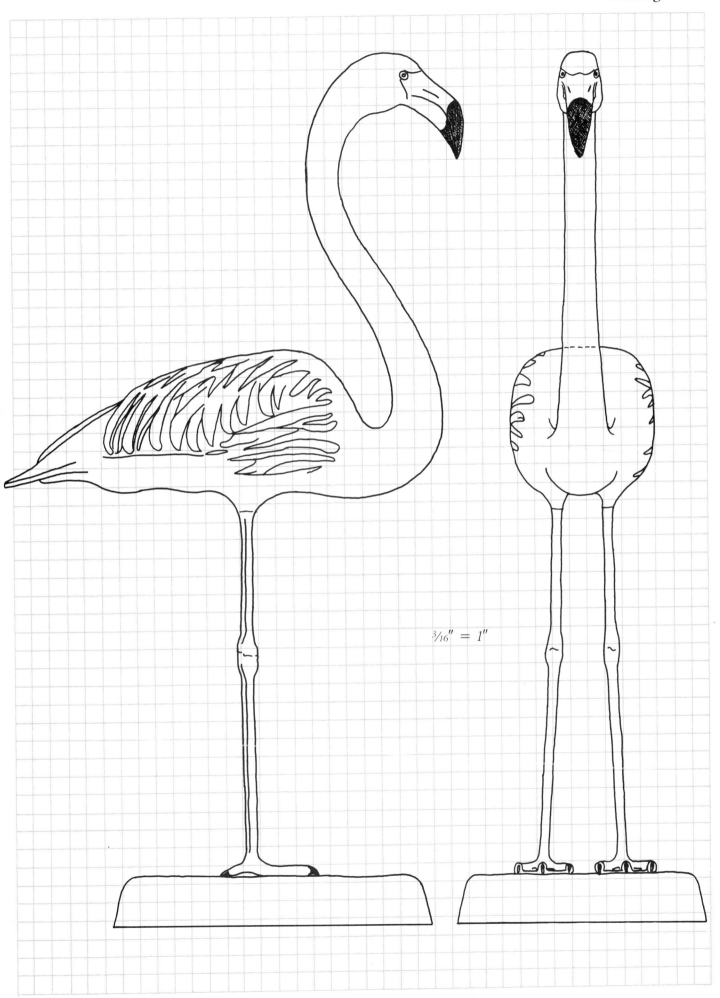

$^{3}/_{16}'' = 1''$

3

MORE ABOUT OWLS

Screech Owls

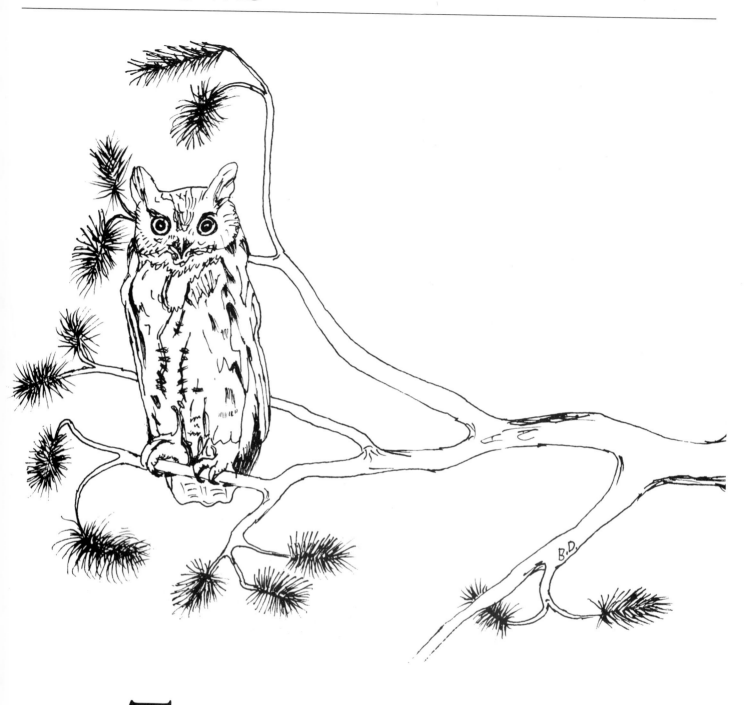

These are small "eared" owls with two color phases which are red and grey. The screech owl feeds on insects, small mammals, fish, crawfish, frogs, lizards, toads, etc. It will usually nest in a hollow of a tree or a nest box.

Illus. 456–457. Owls carved into logs are interesting in themselves or can be used as plant stands or pedestals.

Illus. 458. Owl in turned log is a very interesting weed pot. The same idea could be used to make table lamps.

Illus. 459.   Some easy-to-carve owls for quick projects. Left is a barn owl of cedar, along with two screech owls in staghorn sumac and walnut.

Illus. 460.   Side views.

Illus. 461.   Rear views.

Illus. 462.   Screech owl carved on a 4 × 4 cedar post.

Illus. 463.   Another screech owl carved on top of a round cedar log. Note rough texture showing gouge and chisel marks.

Illus. 464.   Another one-piece owl carved from a tree crotch makes the perfect "y" shape for this piece.

Illus. 465–468.   Views of another screech owl carved from a slightly curved log section.

Illus. 466.   Side view.

Illus. 467.   Rear view.

Illus. 468.   Head close-up. Notice unusual eyes with woodburned shading of the pupils and irises of the eyes and the beak surface.

APPENDICES

METRIC EQUIVALENCY CHART

MM—MILLIMETRES CM—CENTIMETRES

INCHES TO MILLIMETRES AND CENTIMETRES

INCHES	MM	CM	INCHES	CM	INCHES	CM
⅛	3	0.3	9	22.9	30	76.2
¼	6	0.6	10	25.4	31	78.7
⅜	10	1.0	11	27.9	32	81.3
½	13	1.3	12	30.5	33	83.8
⅝	16	1.6	13	33.0	34	86.4
¾	19	1.9	14	35.6	35	88.9
⅞	22	2.2	15	38.1	36	91.4
1	25	2.5	16	40.6	37	94.0
1¼	32	3.2	17	43.2	38	96.5
1½	38	3.8	18	45.7	39	99.1
1¾	44	4.4	19	48.3	40	101.6
2	51	5.1	20	50.8	41	104.1
2½	64	6.4	21	53.3	42	106.7
3	76	7.6	22	55.9	43	109.2
3½	89	8.9	23	58.4	44	111.8
4	102	10.2	24	61.0	45	114.3
4½	114	11.4	25	63.5	46	116.8
5	127	12.7	26	66.0	47	119.4
6	152	15.2	27	68.6	48	121.9
7	178	17.8	28	71.1	49	124.5
8	203	20.3	29	73.7	50	127.0

YARDS TO METRES

YARDS	METRES	YARDS	METRES	YARDS	METRES	YARDS	METRES	YARDS	METRES
⅛	0.11	2⅛	1.94	4⅛	3.77	6⅛	5.60	8⅛	7.43
¼	0.23	2¼	2.06	4¼	3.89	6¼	5.72	8¼	7.54
⅜	0.34	2⅜	2.17	4⅜	4.00	6⅜	5.83	8⅜	7.66
½	0.46	2½	2.29	4½	4.11	6½	5.94	8½	7.77
⅝	0.57	2⅝	2.40	4⅝	4.23	6⅝	6.06	8⅝	7.89
¾	0.69	2¾	2.51	4¾	4.34	6¾	6.17	8¾	8.00
⅞	0.80	2⅞	2.63	4⅞	4.46	6⅞	6.29	8⅞	8.12
1	0.91	3	2.74	5	4.57	7	6.40	9	8.23
1⅛	1.03	3⅛	2.86	5⅛	4.69	7⅛	6.52	9⅛	8.34
1¼	1.14	3¼	2.97	5¼	4.80	7¼	6.63	9¼	8.46
1⅜	1.26	3⅜	3.09	5⅜	4.91	7⅜	6.74	9⅜	8.57
1½	1.37	3½	3.20	5½	5.03	7½	6.86	9½	8.69
1⅝	1.49	3⅝	3.31	5⅝	5.14	7⅝	6.97	9⅝	8.80
1¾	1.60	3¾	3.43	5¾	5.26	7¾	7.09	9¾	8.92
1⅞	1.71	3⅞	3.54	5⅞	5.37	7⅞	7.20	9⅞	9.03
2	1.83	4	3.66	6	5.49	8	7.32	10	9.14

ABOUT THE AUTHORS

Patrick Spielman's love of wood began when, as a child, he transformed fruit crates into toys. Now this prolific and innovative woodworker is respected worldwide as a teacher and author.

His most famous contribution to the woodworking field has been his perfection of a method to season green wood with polyethylene glycol 1000 (PEG). He went on to invent, manufacture, and distribute the PEG-Thermovat chemical seasoning system.

During his many years as shop instructor in Wisconsin, Spielman published manuals, teaching guides, and more than 14 popular books, including *Modern Wood Technology*, a college text. He also wrote six educational series on wood technology, tool use, processing techniques, design, and wood-product planning.

Author of the best-selling *Router Handbook* (over 200,000 copies sold), Spielman has served as editorial consultant to a professional magazine, and his products, techniques, and many books have been featured in numerous periodicals.

This pioneer of new ideas and inventor of countless jigs, fixtures, and designs used throughout the world is a unique combination of expert woodworker and brilliant teacher—all of which endear him to his many readers and to his publisher.

At Spielmans Wood Works in the woods of northern Door County, Wisconsin, he and his family create and sell some of the most durable and popular furniture products and designs available.

Bill Dehos is a wood artist whose work is widely acclaimed for its originality and quality. He is self-taught and has been carving professionally for the past ten years. His keen understanding of nature has contributed to his sensitive interpretations of wildlife, which have won him such an enthusiastic following.

His work has been shown at exhibits and special showings at some of the best galleries in Door County, Wisconsin. He has received many commissions from prominent art lovers. Many of the works that appear here are on exhibition at the Spielmans Wood Works Gallery in Fish Creek, Wisconsin.

Messrs. Spielman and Dehos are presently engaged in preparing a companion volume to this one on the subject of carving life-size wild animals.

Should you wish to write Pat or Bill, please forward your letters to Sterling Publishing Company.

CHARLES NURNBERG
STERLING PUBLISHING COMPANY

CURRENT BOOKS BY PATRICK SPIELMAN

Alphabets and Designs for Wood Signs. 50 alphabet patterns, plans for many decorative designs, the latest on hand carving, routing, cutouts, and sandblasting. Pricing data. Photo gallery (4 pages in color) of wood signs by professionals from across the U.S. Over 200 illustrations. 128 pages.

Gluing & Clamping. A thorough, up-to-date examination of one of the most critical steps in woodworking. Spielman explores the features of every type of glue—from traditional animal-hide glues to the newest epoxies—the clamps and tools needed, the bonding properties of different wood species, safety tips, and all techniques from edge-to-edge and end-to-end gluing to applying plastic laminates. Also included is a glossary of terms. Over 500 illustrations. 256 pages.

Making Country-Rustic Furniture. Hundreds of photos, patterns, and detailed scaled drawings reveal construction methods, woodworking techniques, and Spielman's professional secrets for making indoor and outdoor furniture in the distinctly attractive Country-Rustic style. Covered are all aspects of furniture making from choosing the best wood for the job to texturing smooth boards. Among the dozens of projects are mailboxes, cabinets, shelves, coffee tables, weather vanes, doors, panelling, plant stands and many more durable and economical pieces. 400 illustrations. 4 pages in full color. 164 pages.

Making Wood Decoys. A clear step-by-step approach to the basics of decoy carving. This book is abundantly illustrated with closeup photos for designing, selecting, and obtaining woods; tools; feather detailing; painting; and finishing of decorative and working decoys. Six different professional decoy artists are featured. Photo gallery (4 pages in full color) along with numerous detailed plans for various popular decoys. 160 pages.

Making Wood Signs. Designing, selecting woods, tools, and every process through finishing is clearly covered. Hand-carved, power-carved, routed, and sandblasted processes in small to huge signs are presented. Foolproof guides for professional letters and ornaments. Hundreds of photos (4 pages in full color). Lists sources for supplies and special tooling. 144 pages.

Realistic Decoys. Spielman and master carver Keith Bridenhagen reveal their successful techniques for carving, feather-texturing, painting, and finishing wood decoys. Details that you can't find elsewhere—anatomy, attitudes, markings, and the easy step-by-step approach to perfect delicate procedures—make this book invaluable. Includes listings for contests, shows, and sources of tools and supplies. 274 closeup photos, 28 in color. 224 pages.

Router Handbook. With nearly 600 illustrations of every conceivable bit, attachment, jig, and fixture, plus every possible operation, this definitive guide has revolutionized router applications. It begins with safety and maintenance tips, then forges ahead into all aspects of dovetailing, free-handing, advanced duplication, and more. Details for over 50 projects are included. 224 pages.

Scroll Saw Handbook. This companion volume to *Scroll Saw Pattern Book* covers the essentials of this versatile tool, including the basics (how scroll saws work, blades to use, etc.) and the advantages and disadvantages of the general types and specific brand name models available on the market. All cutting techniques are detailed, including compound and bevel sawing, making inlays, reliefs, and recesses, cutting metals and other nonwoods, and marquetry. There's even a section on transferring patterns to wood! Over 500 illustrations. 256 pages.

Scroll Saw Pattern Book. This companion book to *Scroll Saw Handbook* contains over 450 workable patterns for making wall plaques, refrigerator magnets, candle holders, pegboards, jewelry, ornaments, shelves, brackets, picture frames, signboards, and many more projects. Beginners and experienced scroll saw users alike will find something to intrigue and challenge them. 256 pages.

Working Green Wood with PEG. Covers every process for making beautiful, inexpensive projects from green wood without cracking, splitting, or warping. Hundreds of clear photos and drawings show every step from obtaining the raw wood through shaping, treating, and finishing your PEG-treated projects. 175 unusual project ideas. Lists supply sources. 160 pages.

INDEX